The Definitive Guide to Collecting

Black Dolls

by Debbie Behan Garrett

Published by   Hobby House Press, Inc.
Grantsville, Maryland
www.hobbyhouse.com

DEDICATION

This book is dedicated to the memory of my daddy, Charles Burnett Behan.

To Mama – you are the most faithful, gracious, and elegant woman I know.

To my husband and children: Donnie Garrett, Angela Terry, and Adam Garrett - thank you for understanding my passion.

To my grandson, Marcus "Caleb" Terry - you are my favorite doll baby.

ACKNOWLEDGMENTS

First and foremost I acknowledge my Heavenly Father, Jehovah God. I praise His holy name and I thank Him for giving me the ability to fulfill the promise of this book.

SPECIAL THANKS TO:

Ms. Valerie Ward of New York City, the catalyst for the book becoming a published reality. Thank you, Valerie, for supportively encouraging me to document my extensive Black-doll research and to fulfill my dream of becoming a published author.

To my publisher, Gary Ruddell, thank you for affording me the opportunity to become a published author. To Sherry White, my editor, thank you for your patience and your expertise.

Ms. Debra Richardson, my long-time doll friend – thank you for talking "dolls" with me and for sharing doll ideas and tips.

To those whose names follow the words "courtesy of" throughout the pages of this book – I am truly grateful for the time you spent photographing your dolls and aiding in their descriptions. I deeply regret that I was unable to use each photograph submitted.

Additional copies of this book may be purchased at $27.95 (plus postage and handling) from
Hobby House Press, Inc.
1 Corporate Drive, Grantsville, MD 21536
1-800-554-1447
www.hobbyhouse.com
or from your favorite bookstore or dealer.

©2003 by Debbie Behan Garrett

September 2003

Printed in the United States of America

ISBN: 0-87588-653-1

4   Preface

5   How To Use This Book

6   Chapter 1
Black Dolls - Their Historical and Present-Day Significance
    7   Bisque
    11   Celluloid
    14   Composition
    18   Rubber
    20   Hard Plastic

28   Chapter 2
Cloth Dolls
    28   Artist
    33   Manufactured
    35   Craft, Handmade
    35   Repro, Unmarked

41   Chapter 3
Fashion Dolls

71   Chapter 4
Manufactured Collectible and Play Dolls

101   Chapter 5
Modern Artist Dolls

133   Chapter 6
Personality/Celebrity Dolls

138   Chapter 7
Paper Dolls

146   Chapter 8
Doll Families, Brother and Sister Dolls, Boy Dolls

162   Chapter 9
Dolls as Therapy
    163   "Colorized" Dolls
    163   Kit Dolls
    165   Reborn
    169   Redressed
    167   Restoration
    170   Dolls on Display

174   Index

176   Bibliography

176   About the Author

TABLE OF CONTENTS

Not only did the purchase of *Jessica* spark the author's interest in collecting Black dolls, it led to countless hours of research and study on the subject of Black dolls as well the amassment of over 1000 Black dolls in a personal collection. The research and passion for collecting has culminated in writing this book, *The Definitive Guide to Collecting Black Dolls*. Not your usual doll reference book, the *Definitive Guide* is intended to increase the readers' knowledge of vintage as well as contemporary Black dolls as collectibles and playthings.

Princess House - *Jessica,* 1991
Material: Porcelain, stuffed-cloth body
Height: 16in (40.64cm)
Marks: (Head) Princess House 1991
Hair/Eyes/Mouth: Black curly wig/brown stationary eyes/dimpled cheeks, closed mouth
Clothing: Blue floral dress with lace trim at collar and hem, white pantaloons, white socks, pink ankle strap shoes; pink doll stand
Other: Intended as a gift for her adolescent daughter in 1991, this doll incited the author's passion for Black dolls. Her daughter never received the doll as a gift. This basically nondescript doll remains the first doll in the author's Black-doll collection.
Value: $65

Each photograph contains a description of the featured doll or dolls. The value indicated for each doll is based on dolls in like condition. It is important to note that the value amounts are included as a guide, not as an appraisal of an actual individual doll's value or the amount at which a doll should be purchased or sold. The reader is further reminded that *a doll is only worth the amount that a buyer is willing to pay at a given time*.

Adjectives used to describe the dolls contained within this book and other mentioned dolls include African American, AA, African-American doll, Black, white or Caucasian. Most dolls will be described as Black and the word Black in most cases will be capitalized; however, if a manufacturer has labeled a doll African American or AA, that label is used. The author prefers describing dark skinned dolls as Black.

ABBREVIATIONS

AA = African American or African-American
COA =Certificate of authenticity
LE = limited edition
NRFB = never removed from box
OOAK = one-of-a-kind
VHTF = very-hard-to-find

The intent of this book is to enlighten as well as to entertain the reader. It is hoped that the information and doll photographs will renew your inner child's spirit, will inspire, and/or incite a new interest in Black-doll collecting.

HOW TO USE THIS BOOK

Black Dolls - Their Historical and Present-Day Significance

Dolls are a representation of a people. They depict how we see ourselves and how others see us thereby conveying the values of a society. They teach young people various values from how to be a good parent to racial acceptance. For these reasons, Black dolls are an integral part of our past and present society.

For African-Americans, early handmade dolls made by slaves for their children as well as those that were mass-produced represent the existence of Black people throughout history and the influence they had on our culture. From mammies and cotton pickers to celebrated entertainers and sports figures, from beautiful playthings to collectibles, Black dolls have evolved and are still quite effectual today, albeit in a more positive sense than those of yesteryear.

Because many of the first manufactured Black dolls were not a fair representation of Black people as a whole, many Black collectors do not welcome them into their collections. These dolls were inadequate representations with overly exaggerated features and outrageously dark complexions, but we cannot deny their existence. They are reminders of past painful experiences endured by those who struggled to survive and grasp at a tolerable life. When these dolls are ignored, the past that they represent is also ignored. We cannot deny the existence of the predecessors of today's Black dolls, however painful their reminders. These early dolls should evoke an appreciation of our irrevocable position in today's society. Thankfully, we now have the ability to own more realistic depictions of Black people that are less stereotypical.

Modern Black dolls allow Black children to see themselves in a positive light. They promote self-esteem, self-pride and self-acceptance all of which are important for proper childhood development. Furthermore, Black dolls used as playthings for children of all races can be useful tools to promote diversification and acceptance of others and their differences.

Each of us can affect the history of Black dolls through research. We can also put forth the necessary efforts to ensure that they remain on the doll market. If we cannot create our own, we can certainly pen letters to artists and manufacturers to inform them of the types of Black dolls that are desired. Black people are an important part of our society, and we should be realistically depicted through the continued manufacture of dolls and other playthings.

Bisque dolls consist of an unglazed ceramic, which often results in a gritty texture. These dolls were popular from the mid-1800s through World War I. Dolls made of ceramic date back to the mid-1900s.

Porcelain is the material most often used today and is used for both modern artist dolls and in the reproduction of antique dolls. The porcelain dolls discussed in this chapter are reproductions. Modern porcelain dolls are included in Chapter 5 – Modern Artist Dolls.

Societe Francaise de Fabrication de Bebes et Jouets (SFJB) "Unis France" - Bisque Doll, ca. early 1900s
Material: All bisque
Height: 8½in (21.59cm)
Marks: Head Unis France 60
Hair/Eyes/Mouth: Black, mohair wig/black, glass eyes/open mouth with four teeth, red lip color
Clothing: Multicolored, sewn-on island-style taffeta dress; plaid scarf; beaded necklace
Value: $300

Bisque Baby, ca. late 1940s
Material: Bisque, jointed and strung with cord
Height: 4½in (11.43cm)
Marks: (Back) JAPAN
Hair/Eyes/Mouth: Topknot and two side ponytails/painted eyes/closed mouth
Clothing: Crocheted bonnet, dress and booties
Other: Doll is from collector's childhood
Value: $50
Photograph courtesy of Sheryl A. Van Vleck

Jeannie DiMauro for Premiere Artists Collection - *Lovie*, a Heubach reproduction, ca. 1997
Material: Porcelain with jointed arms, frozen legs
Height: 8in (20.32cm)
Marks: (Signature, edition numbers written on head) Jeannie DiMauro 0137/3000
Hair/Eyes/Mouth: Brown, short curly wig with ribbon accent/brown stationary, side-glancing eyes/closed mouth
Clothing: Ivory dress, lace panties that wrap around doll's hip area
Other: The Heubachs reproduced by Jeannie DiMauro were not originally made as Black dolls. The artist "took a little 'artistic' liberty" to reproduce them as Black dolls.
Value: $50

Jeannie DiMauro for Premiere Artists Collection - *Shellie*, a Hertel, Schwab & Co *Our Fairy* doll reproduction, ca. 1997
Material: Full-body porcelain with jointed arms and legs
Height: 5in (12.7cm)
Marks: (Head) Faintly visible initials HS (Back) artist's signature, written edition numbers - Jeannie DiMauro 0086/1000
Hair/Eyes/Mouth: Brown, painted hair/brown, painted eyes/closed mouth
Clothing: White crocheted short romper, bonnet, and booties
Value: $50

Effanbee Doll Company – *Porcelain Patsy*, reproduction of the 1928 doll, 2001
Material: Full-body porcelain with jointed arms and legs
Height: 14in (35.56cm) on skates; 13in (33.02cm) without skates
Marks: (Head) EFFANBEE PATSY (Back) Effanbee Patsy (stamped) EFFANBEE PATSY DOLL (in the mold)
Hair/Eyes/Mouth: Black, painted hair, two side braids, one top braid/brown, side-glancing eyes/closed mouth
Clothing: Sheer pink dress; off-white, one-piece underwear; white socks and roller skates
Other: This Patsy replica was made from molds taken from an original composition Patsy. Doll is a LE of 1500 worldwide and comes with COA and golden "Patsy by Effanbee" bracelet and doll stand.
Value: $150

1930s Boy and Girl (Reproduction of), 1998
Material: Porcelain
Height: 5½in (13.97cm)
Marks: Unmarked
Hair/Eyes/Mouth: Boy is bald; girl wears scarf/both have painted eyes/red lip color
Clothing: Boy wears reproduction of 1930s shirt, sweater-vest, plaid pants and hat; girl wears red and white checkered mammy type outfit with white apron, red and white polka dot scarf; gold earrings
Value: $50/pair

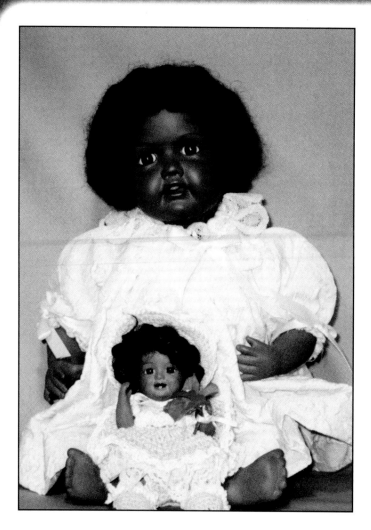

Hilda (Reproduction), ca. 1993; **Little Miss Sunshine** (LMS *Hilda* reproduction), ca. 1996
Material: Full body porcelain
Height: 15in (38.1cm); 6in (15.24cm)
Marks: (Reproduction *Hilda*) DK 1919 (other marks are under wig) Kossi (signature, surname of artist); (*LMS*, head) Patricia Loveless (gold stamped signature) ©1995 (written) 0219
Hair/Eyes/Mouth: (*Hilda*) Hand-made, brown, wavy mohair wig/brown stationary eyes/open mouth with two upper teeth (*LMS*) Brown curly wig/brown stationary eyes; painted upper eyelashes/open mouth with two lower teeth
Clothing: (*Hilda*) Ivory dress with lace collar, lace panties; (*LMS*) yellow and white crocheted dress, panties, bonnet, booties; holds purple flower in left hand
Value: $150 and $60, respectively

Patricia Loveless for Designer Guild, HSN - *Sarah Jane* Reproduction *BeBe*, 1995
Material: Porcelain head, arms, legs; stuffed cloth body
Height: 26in (66.04cm)
Marks: (Head) SFBJ/Paris 11/ Patricia Loveless (signature) 448/2000
Hair/Eyes/Mouth: Brunette curly wig/brown stationary eyes/open-closed mouth, two painted upper teeth
Clothing: Burgundy dress with ivory lace trim, matching hat and drawstring bag; black stockings, brown leatherette shoes; wears gold tone *BeBe* pin at neck of dress
Value: $200

CELLULOID/PLASTIC DOLLS

Celluloid dolls were manufactured from the late 1800s through the 1940s. The manufacture of celluloid dolls was discontinued in the United States due to the material's high flammability. Other countries continued to manufacture and market the dolls. Many of the dolls found today are unmarked; therefore, it is difficult to trace them back to a specific manufacturer and/or date. When a manufacturer's name is unknown, their types and approximate dates of manufacture are indicated.

Rheinische Gummi und Celluloid Fabrik Co. (RGCF)
Negro Doll (possibly *Haiti*), ca. 1930s-1940s
Material: Dark brown celluloid, string-jointed at neck, shoulders and hips; metal eyelids
Height: 18in (45.72cm)
Marks: (Head) Raised turtle within a diamond/with #46 underneath the diamond. (Body) #46
Hair/Eyes/Mouth: Long, black human hair wig, styled in two braids/blue flirty, glass eyes; brown eyelashes/closed mouth
Clothing: Redressed in red, black and brown plaid dress made from a Daisy Kingdom pattern
Other: Doll's right ear is pierced; two center fingers of left hand molded together
Value: $600
Other: In 1930, RGCF registered a design patent for a doll named *Haiti* in brown. Original clothing may have been made of beads, a colorful cotton dress and a straw hat or scarf.
Photograph courtesy of Bonnie Lewis

Boudoir souvenir-type doll, ca. 1940s
Material: Heavy celluloid or plastic head and breast plate; straw-stuffed, mature cotton body, arms and legs
Height: 30in (76.2cm)
Hair/Eyes/Mouth: Molded, black hair/painted eyes/red closed lips
Clothing: Island-style, full-length, yellow print dress with red sash that reads "Miss H..." possibly Miss Haiti; wears combination head scarf/straw hat
Value: $400

Celluloid Baby, Celluloid Kewpie-type girl ca. 1950s
Material: (Left to right) Celluloid with jointed arms and legs, celluloid
Height : (Left to right) 6in (15.24cm); 4½in (11.43cm)
Marks : (Left to right) Unmarked; Made in Japan
Hair/Eyes/Mouth: (Left to right) Molded, painted hair with a hole in head for hair ribbon/side-glancing eyes/closed mouth; hair molded as topknot and on lower portion of head/painted, side-glancing eyes/closed mouth
Clothing: (Left to right) Painted-on clothing; none
Other: Dolls are from owner's childhood
Value: $50 each
Photograph courtesy of Sheryl A. Van Vleck

Celluloid Twins in Bunting, Celluloid Baby, *The Dolly Sisters*, ca. 1930s; 5in (12.7cm), 4in (10.16cm) and 2in (5.08cm).
Marks: (Left to right): Cardboard part of Twins' packaging stamped "Japan," barely visible letters and "UK" on baby's back; *Dolly Sisters* (backs) marked Japan.
Hair/Eyes/Mouth: Bunting twins and Dolly Sisters – molded hair; baby has holes in sides of head for "missing" tufts of hair. All with painted eyes, closed mouths. Twins are nude.
Clothing: Baby wears glued on red and white dress. The five *Dolly Sisters* wear ribbon skirts of different colors.
Values: $75, $50 and $100 respectively

Souvenir Type dolls, ca. 1950s
Material: Celluloid/Plastic
Height: 6, 7, and 9in (15.24, 17.78 and 22.86cm)
Marks: The skirt of one doll has "Martinique" on it, unmarked otherwise
Hair/Eyes/Mouth: (Left and middle) molded hair and eyes. (Right) Plastic, brown stationary eyes. All have closed mouths.
Clothing: Island-style dresses
Value: $35 each

Googly-eyed Doll Pin, ca. 1940s
Material: Plastic, enlarged head; pipe cleaner body
Height: 2in (5.08cm)
Hair/Eyes/Mouth: Hairless/googly eyes enclosed in plastic/painted mouth
Clothing: Blue, plastic grass skirt
Value: $50
Photograph courtesy of Sheryl A. Van Vleck

COMPOSITION DOLLS

Composition dolls were popular during the early 1900s through the early 1950s. Said to be "composed" of unbreakable materials, they were relatively inexpensive to acquire. While they are difficult to break, with time the materials used to construct the dolls (a combination of wood, glue and other materials) deteriorated. This caused the dolls to craze. Fine cracks, flaking, and chips eventually occurred in composition dolls. Today, it is very rare to find a composition doll without any crazing or other flaws. Despite their crazing flaw, composition dolls are highly collectible, vintage dolls.

Most composition dolls were unmarked by their manufacturers. For the composition dolls in this chapter, if the manufacturer's name is known, it is indicated. Otherwise, only the type and approximate year of manufacture are indicated.

American Character - *Debutante*, 1939
Material: Full body composition, heavy walker with walking mechanism and crying mechanism in center of chest
Height: 27in (68.58cm)
Hair/Eyes/Mouth: Replaced black curly wig, brown sleep eyes, open mouth with two upper teeth and two lower teeth, felt tongue, red lip color
Clothing: Redressed in yellow dotted Swiss dress, white socks, white vinyl shoes.
Other: Before purchasing, this doll had been restored and painted black by a prior owner. It is uncertain if American Character originally manufactured this doll as Black.
Value: $500

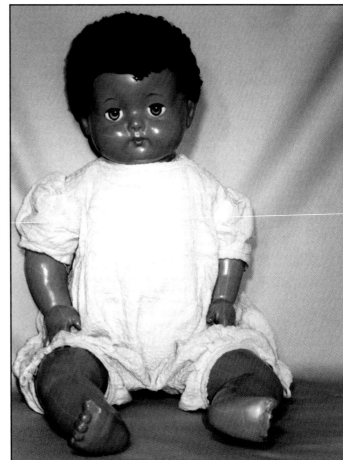

Effanbee - *Sweetie Pie*, 1938-1941
Material: Composition head, arms, legs; stuffed cloth body
Height: 19in (48.26cm)
Marks: (Head) Effanbee
Hair/Eyes/Mouth: Black lamb's wool-type wig/brown sleep eyes/red bow mouth
Clothing: Pink cotton romper
Value: $600

E.I.H., Co. (Horsman) - Compo Boy, ca. early 1900s
Material: Composition head, breastplate, arms, legs, stuffed body with voice box
Height: 12in (30.48cm)
Marks: E. I. H. Inc.
Hair/Eyes/Mouth: Molded hair/painted brown eyes/red bow mouth
Clothing: Blue cotton romper, white leather shoes
Value: $100

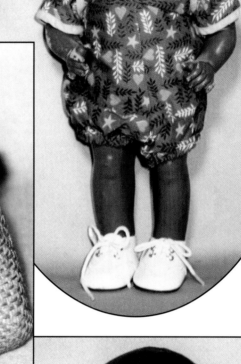

Cotton Pickers, ca. 1936
Material: Composition
Height: 4in (10.16cm)
Marks: Partial hangtag on male reads: Sou.../Texas.../1836"
Hair/Eyes/Mouth: Painted/painted; side-glancing black/open; closed mouths with teeth
Clothing: Original outfits with straw, cotton-filled bags
Other: Dolls were made for a Texas Centennial Celebration in 1936
Value: $250/pair
Photograph courtesy of Cheryl J. Bruce

Composition Boy, ca. early 1900s
Material: All composition with spring-jointed limbs
Height: 9in (22.86cm)
Hair/Eyes/Mouth: Painted black hair/painted black eyes/red bow mouth
Clothing: Red and white cloth romper
Value: $75

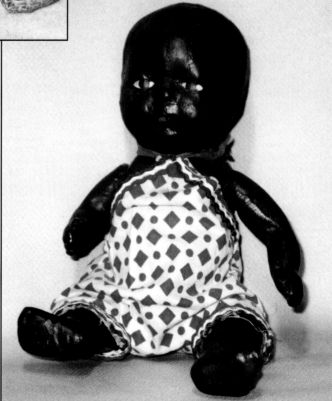

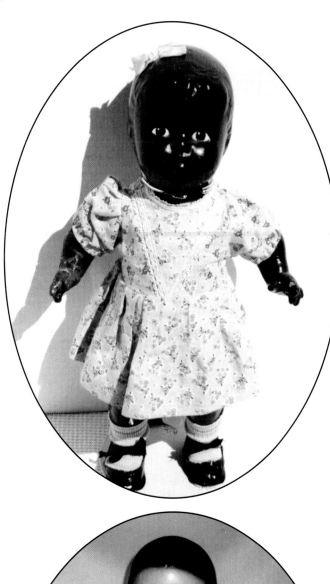

Composition Girl, ca. early 1900s
Material: All composition
Height: 14in (35.56cm)
Hair/Eyes/Mouth: Molded hair/painted brown eyes/closed mouth
Clothing: Cotton dress with attached panties, black leather shoes
Value: $100

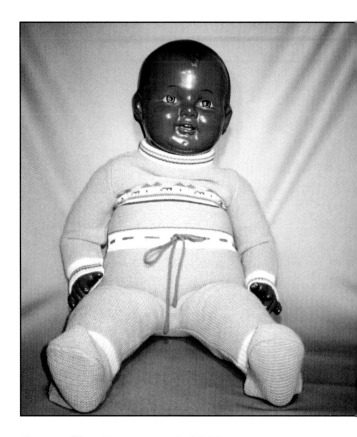

Composition Boy, ca. early 1900s
Material: Composition head, arms, legs, cloth body, voice box
Height: 25in (63.5cm)
Hair/Eyes/Mouth: Molded, black hair/brown sleep eyes with brown eyelashes/open laughing mouth with two upper and two lower teeth, felt tongue
Clothing: Redressed in infant's blue knit romper
Value: $350

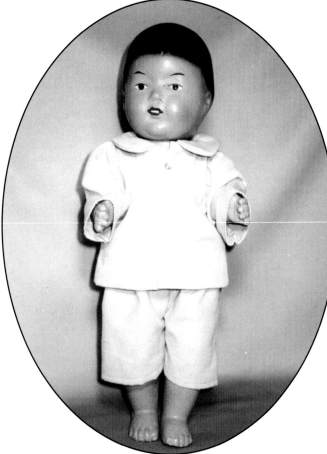

Composition Boy, ca. 1930s
Material: All composition
Height: 14in (35.56cm)
Marks: Barely visible
Hair/Eyes/Mouth: Molded, black hair/painted black eyes/open mouth with painted lips and teeth
Clothing: Redressed in light blue suit
Value: $75

16

Mama Doll, ca. 1930s
Material: Composition head, arms, legs; straw-stuffed body with mama voice mechanism
Height: 25in (63.5cm)
Hair/Eyes/Mouth: Black mohair Shirley Temple-style wig/brown metal sleep eyes/open mouth with two upper teeth, red felt tongue
Clothing: Redressed in child's floral print dress, bonnet, white socks, black leather shoes
Value: $200

Mammy with buggy, ca. early 1900s
Material: Composition head, body, lower arms, and feet. Upper arms are springs. Pushes a metal baby carriage (probably replaced) that contains a plastic Caucasian baby.
Height: 9½in (24.13cm)
Clothing: Molded black hair/painted black eyes/smiling mouth with red lips and painted teeth
Clothing: Wears red and white polka dot dress with matching scarf
Other: Considered to be a pull-toy, *Mammy* was popular from the early 1900s through the 1950s. Effanbee was one of the companies that manufactured this type pull-toy.
Value: $1000

Topsy-type toddler, Topsy-type baby, and Topsy-type circa early 1900s
Material: All Composition
Height: 10in (25.4cm), 12in (30.48cm), and 16½in (41.91cm)
Hair/Eyes/Mouth: Three tufts of hair, otherwise molded/painted side-glancing black eyes/red bow mouth
Clothing: (Left to right) Redressed in aqua dress, peach and white dress, red and white dress
Value: $75 each

Rubber dolls were made from the early 1900s through the 1970s and were relatively inexpensive. The rubber material was considered to be safe for child's play; therefore many children of the 1940s - 1970s owned some type of rubber doll. Collectors of rubber dolls today often are replacing dolls they owned as children or dolls they desired to own.

Sun Rubber - *Amosandra*, ca. 1949; *Tod-L-Tot* and *Sunbabe So-Wee* ca. 1950
Material: Rubber
Height: 10in (25.4cm), 10½in (26.67cm) and 9in (22.86cm)
Marks: *Amosandra*: (Head) ©Amosandra Columbia Broadcasting System, Inc. (Back) Designed by Ruth E. Newton/Manufactured by the Sun Rubber Company/Barberton, OH USA (patent numbers). *Tod-L-Tot*: (On back of molded diaper) Tod-L-Tot. The Sun Rubber Company/Barberton, OH U.S.A. *So-Wee* (Head Sunbabe So-Wee ©Ruth E. Newton/New York, NJ. (Back) Designed by Ruth E. Newton/Manufactured by the Sun Rubber Company/Barberton, OH USA.
Hair/Eyes/Mouth: (All) Molded hair/inset, brown eyes/drinker mouth
Clothing: *Amosandra* and *So-Wee* are redressed. *Tod-L-Tot* has brown molded diaper, socks, and shoes.
Value: $200, $50, $50, respectively

Doll Craftin' - *Craft Boy and Girl*, ca 1960/70s
Material: Rubber or soft vinyl
Height: 12in (30.48cm)
Marks: Faint "Shindana" markings on head; Hong Kong on back
Hair/Eyes/Mouth: (Boy) Molded black curly hair; (Girl) Rooted black hair, two side ponytails/painted eyes/drinker mouth, pink lips
Clothing: Nude
Other: These dolls were the same molds used for the Shindana *Baby Zuri* doll and were probably sold to the Doll Craftin' company by Shindana. They were sold in clear cellophane packages with a cardboard label. The use of the term, "Negro" on their packaging dates them to the late 1960s/early 1970s.
Value: $25 each

Sun Rubber - *Sun Dee* (possibly), ca. 1950s
Material: All rubber
Height: 17in (43.18cm)
Marks: (Head) ©Sun Rubber (Back) Mfg. by the Sun Rubber Co. Barberton Ohio USA (patent information on lower back)
Hair/Eyes/Mouth: Molded, black hair/brown sleep eyes with eyelashes/drinker mouth
Clothing: Redressed in white voile dress
Value: $75

Allied - Girl with molded topknot, ca 1950s
Material: Rubber with jointed arms and legs
Height: 6½in (16.51cm)
Marks: Faintly visible on head: ©Allied (other markings on head are not visible)
Hair/Eyes/Mouth: Molded with topknot curl/painted side-glancing eyes/open mouth
Clothing: Redressed in crocheted dress
Value: $25

Sun Ruco - Viceroy, ca 1930s
Material: Rubber
Height: 11in (27.94cm)
Marks: (Back) A Viceroy Sun Ruco Doll Made in Canada Patent Pending
Hair/Eyes/Mouth: Molded, black hair/brown side-glancing eyes/drinker mouth
Clothing: Redressed in blue crocheted sweater, matching hat, blue overalls
Value: $75

Kewpie-type, ca. 1960s.
Material: Rubber with jointed arms and legs
Height: 14in (35.56cm)
Marks: (Head) 4 (Back) 8/Made in Taiwan
Hair/Eyes/Mouth: Molded top knot, side curls, and one curl in lower back of head/painted black eyes/red lips
Clothing: Red dress with white lace trim at collar and hem
Value: $25

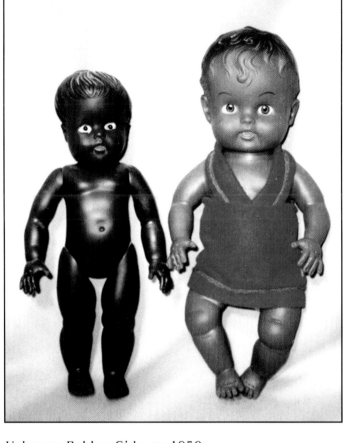

Unknown Rubber Girls, ca 1950s
Material: Rubber and/or soft vinyl
Height: 9½in (24.13cm); 10½in (26.67cm)
Hair/Eyes/Mouth: Smaller doll has molded hair styled in a bun/black beads for eyes (replaced)/open-closed mouth. Other doll has molded curls/brown inset eyes/open-closed mouth.
Clothing: Smaller doll is nude. Larger doll is redressed.
Value: $10 and $15, respectively

HARD PLASTIC DOLLS

Hard plastic dolls were introduced after composition and before Latex and vinyl dolls. These dolls were popular from the 1940s through the late 1950s. Because composition dolls were being manufactured at the time hard plastic dolls were introduced, many manufactures used a combination of composition and hard plastic for their dolls. In this chapter, these are referred to as transitional dolls. This practice continued after Latex (Magic Skin) and vinyl dolls were introduced to the doll market. Many companies manufactured dolls using a combination of hard plastic, vinyl and/or Latex. These are referred to as other transitional dolls.

Hard plastic dolls were virtually indestructible. Many manufacturers used the same molds and many dolls were unmarked. Unfortunately, because of this, it is difficult to identify most hard plastic dolls by name.

Hard plastic dolls had several features that enhanced the imagination of the young child. Those with jointed elbows and/or knees made the dolls appear lifelike in their movements. Sleep eyes gave them a sleep appearance when laid flat. "Ma-ma" criers gave them a voice. Some dolls were given walking mechanisms that allowed their heads to turn as they walked. These are referred to as head-turning walkers.

Hard plastic dolls, because of their durability and added features, were quite popular at the time of their introduction to the doll market and remain highly collectible today.

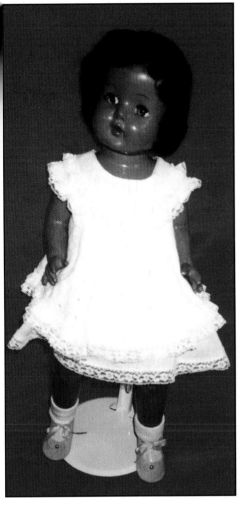

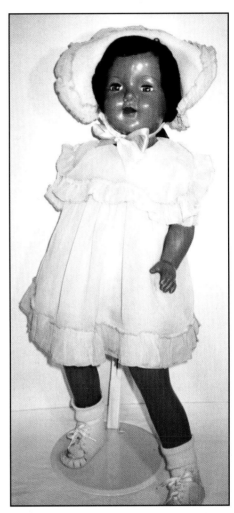

Ma-Ma Doll, ca. 1950s
Material: Hard plastic head and breastplate, stuffed cloth body, composition arms and legs
Height: 21½in (54.61cm)
Hair/Eyes/Mouth: Black, mohair wig/brown sleep-eyes/open mouth with four teeth and felt tongue
Clothing: Redressed in white lace dress with pink cotton under dress; pink faux suede shoes, white socks
Value: $150

Black Shirley Temple-type Child Doll, ca. 1950s
Material: Hard plastic face/ breastplate, stuffed-cloth body, composition arms and legs
Height: 25½in (64.77cm)
Hair/Eyes/Mouth: Black wig styled in loose "Shirley Temple" curls/brown sleep eyes/open mouth with four upper teeth and tongue, red lip color
Clothing: Redressed in red and white checkered dress, white cotton stockings, red shoes
Value: $250

Black Shirley Temple-type Child Doll, ca. 1950s
Material: Hard plastic face/ breastplate; stuffed-cloth body, composition arms and legs
Height: 27in (68.58cm)
Hair/Eyes/Mouth: Black, mohair wig/brown sleep eyes/open mouth with tongue, red lip color
Clothing: Beige organdy dress, matching bonnet, off-white socks; off-white felt, lace-up shoes. (Dress may be original to doll).
Value: $300

Madame Alexander - *Cynthia*, 1949-51
Material: Hard plastic
Height: 14in (35.56cm)
Hair/Eyes/Mouth: Black wig with bangs, original metal hair clips/brown sleep eyes/closed mouth, red lip color
Clothing: Replica blue nylon dress with matching panties; original white socks and black leather shoes
Value: $750

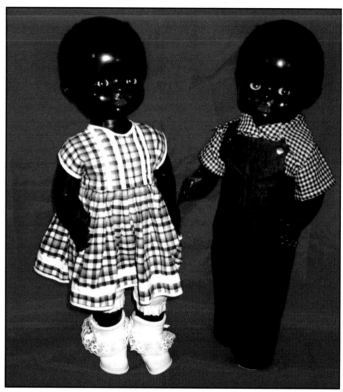

Pedigree-Type Girl and Boy Walkers, ca. 1940s
Material: Hard plastic
Height: 21½in (54.61cm)
Marks: (Head) Made in NZ (New Zealand); grille-type opening on belly; pin-jointed legs
Hair/Eyes/Mouth: Lamb's wool wig/brown flirty sleep eyes/closed mouth, red lip color
Clothing: (Girl) Redressed in blue, white and pink plaid dress, white pantaloons, white lace socks, white vinyl shoes. (Boy) Redressed in blue and white checkered shirt, blue denim overalls, black leather shoes
Other: Lines Brothers of New Zealand, who manufactured Pedigree-type hard plastic walkers, may have manufactured these dolls
Value: $400 each

Left: Rita Walker-type, ca. 1940s
Material: Hard plastic with head-turning mechanism
Height: 25in (63.5cm)
Hair/Eyes/Mouth: Black mohair wig styled in two ponytails/brown sleep eyes/open mouth with four upper teeth and tongue
Clothing: Original tartan plaid dress, white sleeves and mock apron; red vinyl shoes, white rayon socks
Other: Several companies, including Paris Doll Company, manufactured this type doll
Value: $350

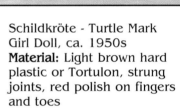

Roberta Walker, 1940s
Material: Hard plastic with head-turning mechanism
Height: 17in (43.18cm)
Marks: Pin-jointed legs
Hair/Eyes/Mouth: Black "Shirley Temple" curled wig/brown sleep eyes/open mouth, four upper teeth, red tongue
Clothing: Redressed in yellow organza dress with yellow satin bow, white socks; original black shoes
Value: $300

Saucy Walker-type dolls, ca. 1950s
Material: Hard plastic
Height: 22½in (57.15cm); 22in (55.88cm)
Marks: None; grille-type opening on belly; pin-jointed legs
Hair/Eyes/Mouth: (Left) Black, short-mohair wig/brown sleep eyes/open mouth with tongue; (Right) Black, mohair wig/brown sleep eyes/open mouth with two upper teeth, red tongue, red lip color
Clothing: (Left) Redressed in aqua dotted Swiss infant's dress, aqua bonnet, white slip, panties, socks and shoes; (Right) period-appropriate, green and white dress; white panties, socks and shoes
Value: $150 each

Schildkröte - Turtle Mark Girl Doll, ca. 1950s
Material: Light brown hard plastic or Tortulon, strung joints, red polish on fingers and toes
Marks: Head: Raised Turtle within a diamond/T 46
Height: 18in (45.72cm)
Hair/Eyes/Mouth: Black, human hair wig styled in two braids/blue glass flirty eyes/closed mouth
Clothing: White cotton, long-sleeve blouse with cuffs and black ribbon bow, burnt orange velvet pants, white leather sandals with metal buckles
Other: "T" mark on Schildkröte dolls indicates the doll is made of Tortulon (a type of plastic). Schildkröte was formerly RGCF and German for Turtle.
Value: $250
Photograph courtesy of Bonnie Lewis

23

Hard Plastic Boy/Man, ca. early 1950s
Material: Hard plastic
Height: 4½in (11.43cm)
Marks: None
Hair/Eyes/Mouth: Black, molded hair/side-glancing eyes/closed mouth
Clothing: None
Other: Doll is from owner's childhood
Value: $50
Photograph courtesy of Sheryl A. Van Vleck

Terri Lee - *Patty-Jo*, 1947-1951
Material: Hard plastic
Height: 16in (40.64cm)
Marks: Body: Terri Lee Patent Pending
Hair/Eyes/Mouth: Black mannequin wig/black painted eyes/closed mouth, red lip color
Clothing: Original red and white check dress with matching panties, replaced white socks and off-white shoes
Other: *Bonnie Lou* is the other Black female in the Terri Lee doll line. *Patti-Jo* can be distinguished from *Bonnie Lou* by her hairstyle of two black ponytails patterned after the cartoon character, *Patty-Jo*, created by African American cartoonist Jackie Ormes. *Bonnie Lou* has brown bob-style wig. The male doll, *Benji*, was the only Black male doll in the Terri Lee line. The Black dolls' eyes are said to glance to the left while the white dolls' eyes (if side-glancing) glance to the right. This, however, may not always be the case since the dolls' features were hand painted, leaving, room for human error.
Value: $1500

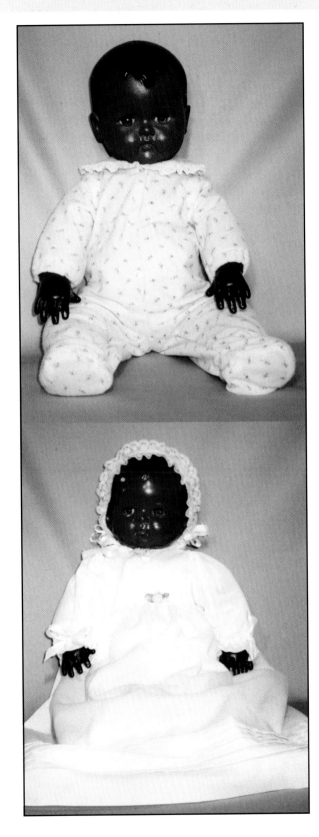

Ideal - *Magic Skin Baby*, Unknown *Magic Skin Baby*, ca. 1940s
Material: Hard plastic, ball-jointed heads with *Magic Skin*, one-piece body, arms and legs
Height: 17in (43.18cm) and 14in (35.56cm)
Marks: (Head, larger doll) 18/Ideal Toys/Made in USA; (head, smaller doll) Made in USA Pat No. 225207
Hair/Eyes/Mouth: Molded, black hair/brown sleep-eyes/closed mouths
Clothing: Redressed in pink pajamas; redressed in white christening gown
Other: The manufacturer of the smaller doll is unknown. *The color authenticity of these dolls is questionable. The *Magic Skin* (Latex) material used for Caucasian dolls darkened (unexpectedly) with time, which caused the dolls to appear Black. Their hard plastic heads remained white. When the darkening occurred, many doll owners painted the dolls' heads brown to match their bodies.
Value: $75 and $60, respectively.

French Child, ca. 1950s
Material: Vinyl head, hard or rigid-plastic body
Height: 12½in (31.75cm)
Marks: (Back) Made in France/France 30 triangle with a Texas-shaped symbol within
Hair/Eyes/Mouth: Black, rooted hair/brown sleep eyes/closed mouth
Clothing: Green and white cloverleaf dress, straw bonnet, white shoes
Value: $50
Photograph courtesy of Linda C. Hayes

Ma-Ma Doll, ca. 1950s
Material: Hard plastic head, stuffed cloth body with working crier, stuffed rubber limbs
Height: 24in (60.96cm)
Marks: Unmarked.
Hair/Eyes/Mouth: Black, mohair wig/brown sleep eyes/open mouth with tongue and two upper teeth, red lip color
Clothing: Pink taffeta period-appropriate dress, matching bonnet; pink, vinyl baby shoes
Value: $150

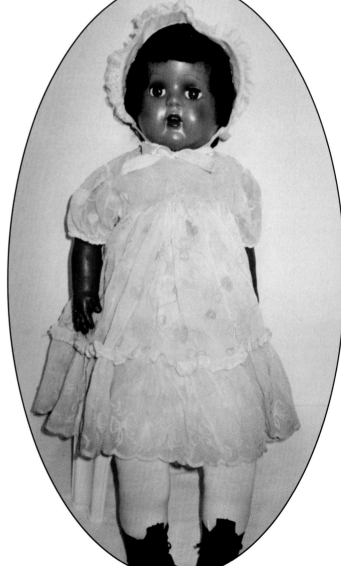

Ma-Ma Doll, ca. early 1950s
Material: Hard plastic head, stuffed cloth body with crier, stuffed Latex (*Magic Skin*) limbs, "Ma-ma" crier or voice box in body
Height: 25in (63.5cm)
Marks: Unmarked
Hair/Eyes/Mouth: Black wig stitched to black netting/brown sleep eyes with light eye shadowing/open mouth with tongue and two upper teeth, red lip color
Clothing: Beige, nylon dress with embroidered flowers; pink taffeta slip, pink panties
Value: $100

(Left to right) Bent Knee Head-Turning Saucy Walker-type; head-turning walker, ca. 1950s
Material: Hard plastic body with vinyl face, head-turning mechanism
Height: 22in (55.88cm) and 23in (58.42cm)
Marks: None; grille-type opening on belly; pin-jointed legs
Hair/Eyes/Mouth: (Left) Long black straight rooted hair with bangs/brown sleep eyes,/closed mouth, pink lip color; (Right) auburn mohair wig styled in two ponytails/brown sleep eyes/closed mouth, coral lip color
Clothing: (Left) Period appropriate pink voile dress, replaced pale blue faux suede shoes, faux pearl necklace; (Right) blue dress with lavender and white checkered collar, mock apron; replaced white stockings and white leather shoes
Value: $200 each

Reproduction Hard Plastic

*L'il Phil/*Black ***Buddy Lee*** (Reproduction of the 1940s doll), 2000
Material: Reproduction hard plastic
Height: 12in (30.48cm)
Marks: None
Hair/Eyes/Mouth: Molded, black hair/painted, side-glancing, black eyes/painted bow mouth
Clothing: Replica of Phillip's 66 hunter green uniform with cap, black belt, black bow tie, black painted-on shoes
Value: $150

CHAPTER 2

Vintage to Modern

Cloth, Cloth-Mixed, and Soft-Sculptured Dolls

Artist Cloth Dolls

Roxann D. Abilogu of Esusu Image African Doll Collection-*NAFU* and *NADIA*, 2001
Material: Soft-sculptured cloth
Height: 6in (15.24cm)
Marks: Signed November 20, 2001
Hair/Eyes/Mouth: (*Nafu*) mohair wig, (*Nadia*) human-type hair/(*Nadia*) painted features, fingernails and toes
Clothing: Elaborate tribal-type clothing
Other: OOAK, anatomically correct, very detailed dolls; soles and palms of feet are a realistic lighter color. *Nafu* (Left) is a male drummer. *Nadia* (Right) is female dancer (*Nafu's* drum sits in front of *Nadia* in photo).
Value: $75 each
Photograph courtesy of Karen Rae Mord

Jane Davies for Deb Canham Artist Designs, Inc.-
Andy Organdy and *Mandy II Organdy*, ca. 1998
Material: Cloth over hard mold, jointed
Height: 5¾in (14.61cm) and 5½in (13.97cm)
Hair/Eyes/Mouth: Hair is plastic or resin molded on heads over fabric/painted facial features
Clothing: Original clothing with very detailed embroidery on *Mandy's* dress
Other: Mandy II is a special LE for UFDC 2002
Value: $110 and $150, respectively
Photograph courtesy of Karen Rae Mord

Ingrid Andrews (San Diego, CA)-*Sister Dolls Ballerina*, 1999
Material: Various textures of cloth; mostly from the Ivory Coast
Height: 30in (76.2cm)
Hair/Eyes/Mouth: Hair is brown, hand-dyed, hand-spun, pure wool partially covered by a scarf/using gold paint, the eyes are painted closed with painted lashes
Clothing: Wears ballerina skirt of burlap with African designs of black, brown and tan; beaded black and tan belt, another belt of macramé tied to skirt with brown cowbell-shaped ornaments. Skirt is lined with orange cotton fabric. The scarf is orange and brown geometric designs, tied in the front with a cowry shell in middle of tie. Wire rim glasses are worn on top of head.
Other: Ms. Andrews, an AA artist, describes her dolls as "Sister Dolls Flippant and Studious African American Cloth Dolls. Sister dolls are never mass produced and are limited in the number created each year".
Value: $150
Photograph courtesy of Bonnie Lewis

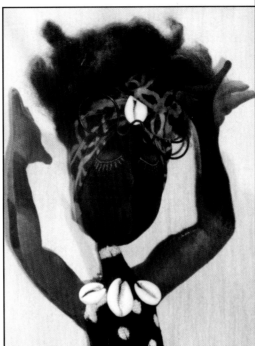

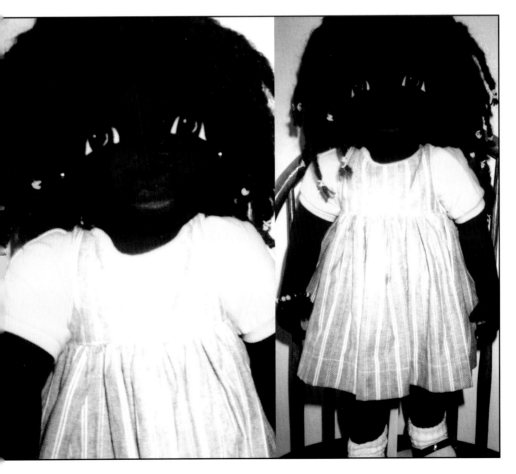

Crafty Sisters of Brooklyn, New York-*Kaila*, ca. 2002
Material: Cloth
Height: 24in (60.96cm)
Hair/Eyes/Mouth: Human-looking hair with individual dreadlocks/ painted eyes/soft-sculptured painted mouth
Clothing: Wears yellow T-shirt; light blue, white and yellow striped dress, white socks, black shoes; wears wooden beaded bracelet
Value: $150
Photograph courtesy of Valerie Ward – NYC

Jean Henderson (Expressions of Color)-
Kacie (KAY-ce), *Loren* (2002), and
Takiyah (2001)
Material: Cloth (Doesuede), fiberfill
stuffing, wooden ball-jointed arms and
legs
Height: 25in (63.5cm)
Marks: signature, date and HEHJEH® on
bottom of foot
Hair/Eyes/Mouth: *(Kacie)* medium brown
synthetic hairpiece/painted dark brown
eyes; *(Loren)* Medium brown synthetic
wig/painted brown eyes/closed mouth;
(Takiyah) synthetic black braids/black
painted eyes
Clothing: All dolls wear original outfits
designed by artist and pedicures.
Takiyah wears sandals; *Kacie* and
Loren's feet are bare
Value: $400 (*Kacie* and *Loren*), $375
(*Takiyah*)
Photograph courtesy of Jean Henderson

Mari Morris-*Donna* (One-of-a-Kind), 2001
Material: All cloth
Height: 15½in (39.37cm) in permanent
crossed-leg seated position
Marks: Artist's signature on bottom with the
year 2001; Skirt label reads: "The Tickles
Collection Mari Morris Altadena Ca."
Hair/Eyes/Mouth: Brown, rooted dreadlocks
adorned with cowry shells/painted, brown
eyes and facial features
Clothing: Animal print halter that ties behind
neck, black sheer skirt with stitched gold
vertical stripes; upper skirt made of gold
beads, sequins and gold tassels. Gold bead
adorns belly button. Wears blue beaded
anklet and white, sheer scarf draped around
arms.
Other: Anatomically correct; individually
stitched fingers and toes with red polish.
There are different versions of this doll with
different names, clothing and hairstyles.
Value: $275
Photograph courtesy of Bonnie Lewis

William Tung, Treasures Forever
Collection for Home Shopping
Network - *Faye Frumpkin*, 1993.
Material: Velour-type cloth
Height: 23in (58.42cm)
Marks: 550/2500 written on stomach
Hair/Eyes/Mouth: Black yarn styled in
two ponytails/solid black plastic
eyes/stitched nose and mouth
Clothing: Multicolored orange and
green dress, orange socks, white
vinyl sneakers with Velcro closure
Other: All of the *Frumpkins'* names
begin with the letter, "F". This is the
only Black *Frumpkin* doll sold
through HSN
Value: $50
*Photograph courtesy of Angela
Garrett Terry*

Norah Wellings-**Islander doll**, ca. 1930s
Material: Stuffed velvet
Height: 14in (35.56cm)
Marks: (Foot tag) "Made in England by Norah Wellings"
Hair/Eyes/Mouth: Black mohair wig/side-glancing black glass eyes/red painted nostrils and lips, white painted teeth
Clothing: Orange and wheat-colored grass skirt, orange arm bracelet, straw wrapped around legs
Value: $250

Norah Wellings trio, ca. 1930s
Material: Stuffed velvet
Height: (Left to right) 13in (33.02cm), 11in (27.94cm) and 10in (25.4cm)
Marks: Larger and mid-size dolls have tag on left foot, "Made in England by Norah Wellings." Smaller doll's tag is on right foot
Hair/Eyes/Mouth: Larger doll has reddish-brown mohair wig; smaller dolls have brown mohair wigs/painted eyes/painted mouths with teeth
Clothing: Brown and velvet trousers, rust and brown velvet trousers, gold & brown velvet trousers
Value: $275, $250, $225, respectively
Photograph courtesy of Valerie Ward – NYC

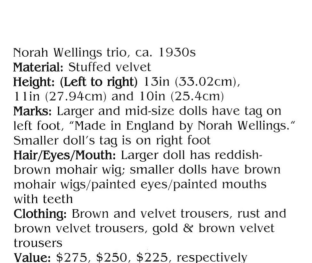

Babyland General Cabbage Patch Kids (CPK) - *Georgiana*, 1986 Southern Bell Edition
Material: Soft-sculptured cloth
Height: 22in (55.88cm)
Marks: (Body Tag) Cabbage Patch Kids, the Little People from Babyland General, Xavier Roberts, ©1978, 1980, 1981, 1983 Original Appalachian Artworks, Inc. Cleveland, OH 30528 All Rights Reserved. Xavier Roberts' gold signature on bottom of doll's left foot.
Hair/Eyes/Mouth: Brown yarn hair styled in two ponytails/brown eyes/closed mouth
Clothing: All original outfit
Value: $400

Dolls from Kenya, ca. 1990s
Material: Cloth, yarn, felt
Height: 7½in (19.05cm)
Marks: Hangtag: "Dolls from Kenya"
Hair/Eyes/Mouth: Yarn hair with braids and beads/felt eyes/felt mouths
Clothing: Authentic Kenyan fabric, gold tone necklace and bracelet
Value: $25 each

European Toy Collection-Unicef Kids United States of America *Laurie* and Tanzania *Moza*, 1991
Material: Cloth
Height: 14in (35.56cm)
Marks: (Body tags) US Committee for Unicef European Toy Collection Portage, IN 46368
Hair/Eyes/Mouth: Black yarn hair/screen printed facial features
Clothing: All original outfits
Other: *Laurie*: Comes with booklet that contains doll's bios and USA trivia questions and answers. *Moza*: Booklet contains doll's bios and Swahili-Tanzania Greetings and Pronunciation Guide
Value: $45 each

Horsman-*Althea Babyland Rag Doll*, 1997
reproduction of original 1930s doll
Material: Cloth
Height: 15in (38.1cm)
Marks: (Body marks) "97-10616 *Babyland
Ragdoll Althea,* ã1997 Horsman, Div. of
Gatabox Ltd., New York, NY 10010"
Hair/Eyes/Mouth: Brown curly bangs
underneath a red head scarf/brown
eyes/screen-painted red lips
Clothing: Original outfit
Other: COA indicates this doll is one of 3000
pieces, numbered limited edition
Value: $75

Faith Ringgold/Merry Makers, Inc.-*Cassie From
Tar Beach*, 1994
Material: Cloth with yarn hair
Height: 14in (35.56cm)
Marks: (Body tag) "Cassie From Tar Beach 1994,
1991, Faith Ringgold"
Hair/Eyes/Mouth: Yarn hair/painted side-glancing
eyes/painted lips
Clothing: Original clothing
Other: Faith Ringgold is an AA author of
children's books. Cassie is the main character
in Ms. Ringgold's multiple-award winning book,
Tar Beach. A mini hard cover edition of the
Caldecott Honor Book is included with doll.
Value: $35

Swansea Dolls Distributed by Gibson
Greeting Company-*Kwanzaa Dolls*, 2001
Material: Brown velour faces, hands and
legs; brown, stuffed-cloth body
Height: 14in (35.56cm)
Marks: Label on foot with manufacturer's
name and care instructions
Hair/Eyes/Mouth: Black yarn hair/
embroidered eyes/embroidered nose
and red lips
Clothing: All original outfits
Value: $25 each
Photograph courtesy of Freda Goldston

Beloved Belindy (handmade), 1995
Material: Stuffed brown cloth head, body, and arms; legs are red and white striped material
Height: 25in (63.5cm)
Hair/Eyes/Mouth: Button eyes, painted red nose, white mouth
Clothing: Wears red kerchief on head; red and white dress with white pantaloons, red cloth shoes
Value: $50

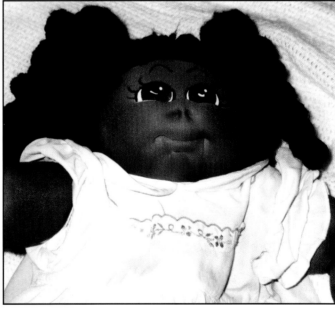

Cabbage Patch Kid-type
Material: Dark brown needle-sculptured face, nylon stuffed-body, sculptured arms, legs and belly button
Height: 18in (45.72cm)
Hair/Eyes/Mouth: Black yarn, braided hair/hand-painted eyes/needle-sculptured nose and lips
Clothing: Blue and white dress, white socks; handmade by collector's sister-in-law
Value: $50
Photograph courtesy of Freda Goldston

Black Americana Girl, ca. 1940s-1950s
Material: Stuffed brown cloth
Height: 23in (58.42cm)
Hair/Eyes/Mouth: Black yarn hair/felt eyes and exaggerated red felt mouth
Clothing: Red dress
Value: $75

Cloth Boy and Girl, 1995
Material: Cloth
Height: 8in (20.32cm)
Hair/Eyes/Mouth: Yarn hair/screen-painted faces
Clothing: (Boy) brown and white suspender pants; (girl) ivory cotton dress
Other: Girl is holding a 3in (7.62cm) composition doll
Value: $30 (cloth pair), $15 (mini composition doll)

Cloth Girl Doll with Baby Doll, ca 1990s
Height: 29in (73.66cm) and 14in (35.56cm)
Hair/Eyes/Mouth: (Larger) black yarn hair knotted in four yarn braids/embroidered eyes/embroidered mouth, nose; (smaller) mohair wig/embroidered eyes/soft-sculptured nose and mouth
Clothing: Dressed by unknown doll maker
Value: $50 and $25, respectively
Photograph courtesy of Debra Richardson

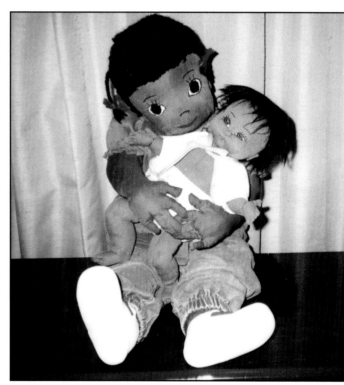

Cloth Girl Doll with Doll, ca. 1990s
Height: 9½in (24.13cm) and 3½in (8.89cm)
Marks: Larger doll's pantaloons signed by "Eleanor Todd"
Hair/Eyes/Mouth: Yarn hair/painted eyes/painted nose and mouth
Clothing: Red and white gingham dress with white pinafore and pantaloons, red felt shoes; dolly wears red and white gingham dress
Value: $20

Nut Head Family, ca. 1920s
Material: Cloth with heads made of nuts
Height: (Mother and father; children)
6in (15.24cm); 3½in (8.89cm)
Hair/Eyes/Mouth: Fibrous black material, matted and glued to heads/painted features
Clothing: Original clothing
Value: $300 (the group)
Photograph courtesy of Cheryl J. Bruce

Oil Cloth Doll, ca 1930s
Height: 12in (30.48cm)
Hair/Eyes/Mouth: Yarn bangs, rest of head covered with scarf/painted side-glancing eyes/painted mouth
Clothing: Sewn-on multicolored top, brown sewn-on pants. Top's fabric used to cover feet
Value: $75

Cloth Folk Art Woman and Man, ca. 1930s
Height: 9¹/8in (23.18cm)
Hair/Eyes/Mouth: Sewn-on gray-white thread-type hair under scarf and hat/painted eyes/closed mouths
Clothing: Original clothing
Other: Wired arms and legs
Value: $250
Photograph courtesy of Cheryl J. Bruce

Souvenir Dolls, ca. 1990s
Height: (Left to right) 8in (20.32cm), 10in (25.4cm), 9in (22.86cm) and 6in (15.24cm)
Clothing: Dolls wear Caribbean Island-type clothing. The doll on the far right is an angel, wears black and red polka dot romper and has black wings.
Value: $15-25

Souvenir Dolls, ca. 1970s
Material: Cloth and porcelain
Height: (Left to right) 9in (22.86cm), 14in (35.56cm) and 15in (38.1cm)
Marks: Puerto Rico written on middle doll's hat; others are unmarked
Hair/Eyes/Mouth: None have hair; painted/side-glancing eyes/closed mouths
Clothing: All wear Caribbean Island-type, stitched-on clothing
Value: $35-75

Victorian Paper Company - Reproduction
Topsy Turvy *Prissy & Missy*, 1998
Material: All cloth body with handless arms
Height: 13in (33.02cm)
Marks: (Skirt tags - front) "Made exclusively for Victorian Paper Co. by Pockets of Learning." ©1998/ Made in Philippines
Hair/Eyes/Mouth: Scarves cover heads/embroidered eyes/painted lips
Clothing: *Prissy* wears black, red, maroon and yellow print skirt. *Missy's* skirt is blue flower print on brown/beige background.
Value: $50
Photograph courtesy of Bonnie Lewis

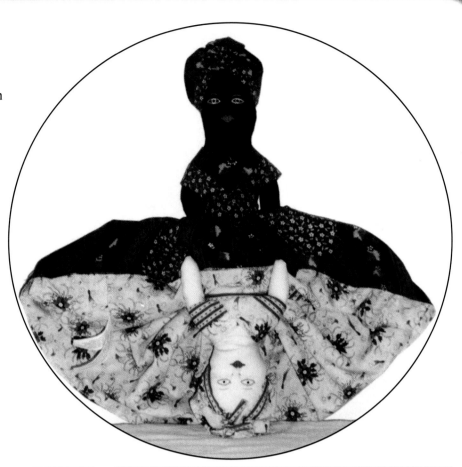

Toaster Cover Dolls, ca. 1950s
Material: cloth/cardboard
Height: 14in (35.56cm), 20in (50.8cm)
Hair/Eyes/Mouth: Smaller doll has painted features/larger doll has button eyes/stitched mouth
Clothing: Both wear headscarves and cotton print dresses with aprons
Value: $25 and $50

Topsy Turvy Dolls, ca. 1980s
Material: Cloth
Height: 15in (38.1cm) and 5in (12.7cm)
Marks: Larger doll is handmade with "Jamaica" stitched on skirt; smaller doll was made in Taiwan, MidWest Importers
Hair/Eyes/Mouth: Yarn hair/larger doll has painted features; smaller doll has stitched eyes/no nose or mouth
Clothing: Larger doll (awake side) pink print dress; (sleeping side) white dress. Smaller doll (black doll side) red with white polka dots, white apron; (white doll side) white with red polka dots, red skirt. larger doll is black on both sides. The smaller doll is white on one side and black on the other
Value: $25 and $5

Fashion Dolls

asha

nichelle

CHRISTIE.

Most every little girl, young and old, has owned a *Barbie*® doll (and/or one of her friends.) This chapter is devoted to those who continue to collect 11½-in (29.21cm) fashion dolls and the larger fashion dolls that have emerged since the *Barbie*® doll's inception. Because the *Barbie*® doll sets the trend for American fashion-doll collectors, this chapter will begin with *Barbie*® and her friends.

For NRFB dolls, only the box date is given. Typically, dolls were introduced to the doll market one year after the box date. NRFB dolls' marks are not indicated.

The Faces of Black *Barbie*®

Where possible, the face mold used for each Black Barbie® doll or friend is indicated. The "vintage *Christie*®" face mold refers to the face similar to *Midge*® used for the 1970s dolls. The *Steffie*® face mold was used on the first Black Barbie in 1979/80. The "Hispanic" mold was used in the late 1970s – 1987. The "new" *Christie*® face mold refers to the *Christie*® face used from approximately 1988 on, after Mattel™ discontinued the use of the "Hispanic" mold. The *Asha*®, *Shani*®, and *Nichelle*® face molds or variations thereof refer to molds used in the mid-1990s through the publication of this book. The *Teresa*® face has been used since the 1990s on both AA and Hispanic dolls. The Mackie-face mold from the 90s continues to be used today. *Fantasy Goddess of Africa*™ mold is abbreviated FGOA.

40th Anniversary Ken® and Barbie® dolls, 2001 and 1999, respectively, (*Nichelle*® and *Jamal*® molds) commemorates *Ken*® and *Barbie*® doll's 40th year on the doll market.
Value: $60 each

Avon™ Representative Barbie®, 1998, (*Nichelle*® mold), yellow jacket, black straight skirt, black hose and shoes, golden stud earrings, yellow Avon™ shopping bag. Hair is styled in short curly "afro".
Value: $75

Byron Lars Runway Collection™ - In the Limelight™ Barbie®, 1997, the first in the series, (*Nichelle®* mold), wears chocolate brown gown with brown and silver lamé coat with faux fur trim at collar and wrists; has lime green lining. Faux diamond earrings and a faux diamond pin at collar accent her outfit and chocolate brown high-heel shoes. Black hair is styled in an upswept hairdo. Includes doll stand, COA. Mr. Lars is an AA New York fashion designer.
Value: $250
Close-up photograph courtesy of Freda Goldston

Byron Lars Runway Collection™ - Cinnabar Sensation®, 1998, the second in the series, (*Asha*® mold), wears cinnamon color blouse with laced closure, cinnamon and gold brocade skirt; full-length taffeta coat with marabou feather trim, black shoes. Upswept rooted brown hairstyle is accented with beads. Doll stand, COA.
Value: $150

Byron Lars Runway Collection™ - Plum Royale™, 1999, the third in the series, (*Shani*® mold), dress has aqua bodice with plum and mauve trim, satin plum skirt with intricate lace overlay. Full-length, plum velvet coat has faux diamond button closure from the waist down, exaggerated sleeve length with faux fur trim at wrists. Coat lined in aqua lamé; aqua, gold and plum-embroidered embellishments and beads on back hem match those on outer collar of coat. Upswept rooted black runway hairstyle; black shoes, doll stand, COA.
Value: $150

Byron Lars Runway Collection™ - Indigo Obsession™, 2000, the fourth in the series, (*FGOA* mold). Wears indigo-blue silk shantung suit (jacket and full-length skirt). Jacket has faux diamond button closure and one faux diamond accents each pocket. The long sleeves have a large silver lamé cuff. The flared skirt is embellished with embroidered pastel flowers and faux diamonds atop a peach silk trim and faux gray fur at hem. Doll holds a faux gray fur muff. Doll's platinum blonde, cropped hair with side part is a striking contrast to her deep dark brown skin color; has doll stand and COA.
Value: $150

Byron Lars Treasures of Africa™, Moja™,
2001, first in the series, (*FGOA* mold). *Moja™*,
which means one in Swahili, has an elaborate
headdress, wears a brown coat with beaded
brown midriff top, graduated brown-to-gold
shimmering pants with a slight flare leg, gold
shoes, rows of gold tone necklaces, faux ivory
and gold tone upper arm bracelets. Hands and
forearms bear gold tribal tattoos.
Value: $150

Byron Lars Treasures of Africa™, Mbili™, 2002,
second in the series. *Mbili™*, which means two
in Swahili, has a full head of natural afro-shaped
hair, the front of which is pulled back and
adorned with beads; wears beaded hoop
earrings. Elaborate gown has backless knit
sweater with beaded corset, white and black
feather train on the multicolored skirt and blue
high-heel boots; has doll stand, COA.
Value: $150

Byron Lars Treasures of Africa™, Tatu™, 2003,
third in the series, (no photograph available),
has *FGOA* face, with lighter vinyl.

Classique Collection™ Evening Extravaganza™ Barbie®, 1993, first black doll in series, ("new" *Christie®* mold), wears shimmering gold and yellow gown designed by AA fashion designer, Kitty Black-Perkins. Gold shoulder gloves, beaded earrings, and gold shoes complete her outfit.
Value: $125

Classique Collection™ Starlight Dance™ Barbie®, 1996, (*Nichelle®* mold), wears white satin gown with silver embellishments on bodice/back of skirt. Gown designed by Cynthia Young. Has upswept hairdo.
Value: $85

Diva Collection™ - Gone Platinum™ Barbie®, 2001, (*Shani* mold), platinum blonde hair with golden highlights; wears silver gown with silver, full-length gloves, gray shoes; has COA, doll stand.
Value: $50

46

Dolls of the World® - *Nigerian, Jamaican, Kenyan* and *Ghanian Barbie®* 1989, 1991, 1993, and 1996, respectively. "New" *Christie®* mold (*Nigerian* and *Jamaican*), *Nichelle®* and *Shani®* face (*Kenyan* and *Ghanian*). Dolls wear outfits inspired by the countries they represent. Boxes contain information regarding the represented countries.
Value: $75 each

Dolls of the World® - *Princess of South Africa™ Barbie®*, 2002, the most recent Black *Barbie®* DOTW. Doll wears Ndebele tribe-inspired outfit. (No photograph available at time of publication.)
Value: $30

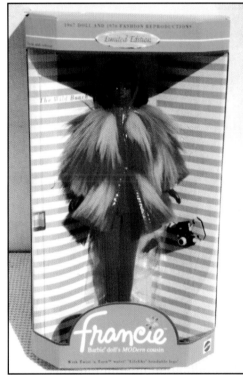

Francie®, Wild Bunch™ - Barbie® doll's MODern cousin, (*Francie®* mold) a reproduction doll wearing reproduction of 1970 *Wild Bunch* outfit; brown hair with bangs, painted brown eyes; colorful orange outfit with orange boots and camera.
Value: $75

Free Moving™ Curtis® and *Cara®*, 1974. *Curtis®* (*Brad®* mold); *Cara®* (*Steffie®* mold); push-button in back makes dolls move in action poses.
Value: $75 each

Harley-Davidson™ Barbie® #5, the final and only Black doll in the five-doll series, (*Asha*® mold), wears black faux leather Harley-Davidson™ biking outfit with helmet and backpack, gold tone earrings, black shades; has rooted black hair styled in multiple tiny braids.
Value: $150

Millennium Princess™ Barbie®, 1999 (*Nichelle*® face), brunette hair, wears silver crown, royal blue velvet gown with silver trim in middle of skirt, bodice, cuffs, and sleeves. Keepsake Happy New Year 2000 ornament included.
Value: $50

Happy Holidays® *Barbie*® *dolls*: First and last in the *Happy Holidays*® series, 1990 and 1998, respectively. Face molds: "New" *Christie*® and *Nichelle*®, respectively. The 1990 doll is the only doll that came with an ornament inside the box. All other versions had separately sold ornaments. The separately sold *1998 Keepsake Ornament* is pictured.
Value: $75 and $150, respectively; ornament $10

48

Island Fun™ Christie® and Island Fun™ Steven®, 1987, ("new" Christie® and Steven® molds), both wear beach attire. Christie® has brown rooted hair. Steven® has molded hair. According to survey, the Steven® face mold is considered the most handsome of the 1980s-2002 male face molds used for the Black male dolls in the Barbie® line. As a contrast, the "new" Christie face mold is one of the least popular face molds used for Black Barbie® and friends.
Value: $20 each

Ruby Radiance Barbie®, the Jewel Essence Collection, 1996, Bob Mackie design, (Nichelle® mold), wears ruby red velvet gown with faux ruby and diamond embellishments at bodice, matching ruby red velvet head wrap. Ruby red satin fabric outlines bodice and back of gown. Wears faux diamond and ruby earrings, red shoes. Brown rooted hair is styled in an upswept hairdo, comes with doll stand and COA.
Value: $100

Silkstone Lingerie Barbie®, 2002, Fashion Model Collection with "genuine" Silkstone body 2002. First African American or black doll with the vintage Barbie® face, wears a sheer black bustier with pink bow accent, matching short robe, black nylon hose and black heels, gold tone dangle earrings. Black hair styled in a modern bob with side-swept bangs; has painted-brown, side-glancing eyes, beauty mark on left cheek, dark red lip and nail color, comes with stand.
Marks: (Head) © Mattel™ 1958. (Back) ©1991-2000 Made in China. This doll is the fifth in the Silkstone Lingerie Barbie® series and the only African American doll included at time of printing.
Value: $75

Midnight Tuxedo™ Barbie®, 2001, Mattel's first African-American Club *Barbie*® doll. (*FGOA* mold), brunette hair, wears black, full-length, sleeveless, double-breasted (tuxedo-style) gown with black faux fur stole.
Value: $350
Photograph courtesy of Melodie Anderson

MEMBERS' CHOICE™
2001
Two Thousand One
EDITION
Midnight Tuxedo™ Barbie®

Starlight Splendor™, Bob Mackie design, 1991, ("new" *Christie*® face), wears white and black beaded gown trimmed with feathers and sequins and sequin-trimmed headdress, heavy eye makeup.
Value: $700
Photograph courtesy of Valerie Myers

Popular Vintage *Barbie*® Friends/Family
***Talking Brad*®**, 1969 (*Christie*® doll's boyfriend).
Bendable legs.
Value: $100
***Live Action™ Christie*®**, 1970. *Midge*® face, rooted
eyelashes, twist and turn body; wears colorful 1970s
outfit.
Value: $150
***Malibu Christie*®**, 1975, one of the most popular
1970s dolls. Has the vintage *Christie* face and very
dark skin coloring.
Value: $50
***Black Barbie*®**, 1979, designed by African American
designer, Kitty Black-Perkins, first black doll that
was actually named *Barbie*®. All other 11½in
(29.21cm) Mattel™ Barbie® family black dolls prior to
this time were friends of *Barbie*®, never given the
actual Barbie® name. Doll has *Steffie*® face mold,
wears a red bodysuit with wrap and snap skirt; red
shoes, red earrings. Comes with afro pick.
Value: $75
***Sunsational Malibu™ Christie*®**, 1981 (box date), has
the Hispanic face mold. The front and back of box
show a Black doll with the *Steffie*® face.
Value: $50
***Sunsational Malibu™ Ken*®**, 1981, aka "rooted hair
Ken®." The first black *Ken*® doll with rooted hair.
Value: $50

***Sydney 2000 Olympic Pin Collector Barbie*®**, 1999,
Nichelle® face mold, wears khaki hat and vest with
mock pins, blue pants, tan and white shoes, khaki
and blue handbag; stand and official Sydney 2000
Olympic pin included.
Value: $50

51

Shopping Chic™, 1995, designed exclusively for Spiegel™, (*Asha®* mold), wears leopard print hat, black satin jacket with leopard-print trim at collar and cuffs, leopard-print handbag, gold skirt, gold earrings, black shoes, black stand. Comes with black French poodle and golden leash.
Value: $75

Tangerine Twist™ Barbie® - *Fashion Savvy Collection*, 1997, (*Nichelle®* mold), the first doll in this African-American-only doll series, designed by Kitty Black-Perkins "to celebrate the unique style, image and opulence" of the AA woman; wears satin tangerine suit, leopard print hat, black gloves, black hand bag, orange shoes.
Value: $75

United Colors of Benetton™ Christie®, 1990, ("new" *Christie®* face), wears multicolored knit top, pants, jacket, matching hand bag designed by Kitty Black-Perkins. Black rooted hair is styled in two sections that contain multiple twists; comb and brush included.
Value: $50

Uptown Chic™, the second doll in the *Fashion Savvy Collection*, 1998, (*Teresa®* mold), a Kitty Black-Perkins fashion design; short cropped black afro, wears golden glasses, golden earrings, purple double-breasted jumpsuit accented by multicolored scarf, carries yellow snakeskin shoulder bag and holds cell phone. Yellow wide-brimmed hat and black shoes complete the look.
Value: $75

Very Velvet™ Christie®, 1998, (*Asha®* mold), wears purple gown; comes with three sticker sheets and three markers to apply color/designs to doll's dress.
Value: $35

WNBA™ Christie®, 1998, ("new" *Christie®* mold) wears replica of WNBA outfit; comes with basketball and COA. Picture of Rebecca Lobo on front of box.
Value: $40

Other 11½-in (29.21cm) Fashion Dolls by Mattel™

Asha®, *African American Collection Special Edition*, first, second, and third edition. Box dates: 1994 first and second edition; 1995 third edition. Dolls wear afrocentric attire and have *Shani*® face mold.
Value: $40 each

Shani® and her friends, *Asha*® and *Nichelle*®, 1991. Dolls wear brilliantly colored, glittery gowns that become mini dresses and jackets.
Value: $75 each

Shani® doll's boyfriend, *Jamal*®, introduced the "*Jamal*®" face mold, 1991. Stands 12in (30.48cm), has mustache and molded black hair, wears a yellow linen-like party tux that transforms into a casual outfit. Brown shoes and white socks and brown attaché case included.
Value: $75

Soul Train™ Shani®, Soul Train™ Jamal®, Soul Train™ Asha® and Soul Train™ Nichelle®, 1993.
Value: $50 each

Other 11½in - 12in (29.21cm - 30.48cm) Fashion Dolls

Alysa® - Simply Chic, Tropical - Integrity Toys™, 2000 designed by Jason Wu, wears pale pink silk-like strapless dress with faux diamond and silver beaded pin; faux pearl necklace, bracelet, and ear studs; black heels, full-length gloves; has rooted auburn ponytail, green painted eyes. Personalized hatbox and doll stand included.
Marks: Integrity Toys, 1996 on head
Value: $45

Candi® - Dolls by Helene Hamilton, an AA doll designer and Charisse® by Mikelman
Candi® Couture, ca. 1994. Doll wears black spandex "catsuit" with Candi Couture on bodice, pink high heels. Brown, rooted hair is styled in a braided ponytail, accented by a black satin ribbon.
Marks: Hamilton Toys Inc, ©1990.
Value: $50
Honey Candi®, ca. 1998, wears St. Tropez separates outfit - peach satin short-sleeve top and pants, peach shoes, straw hat with peach and pink ribbon "flowers." Long, auburn hair is rooted. Eyes are painted green.
Marks: Hamilton Toys Inc, ©1990
Value: $50
Candi® Girl, ca. 1997. Doll wears red spandex dress, red heels. Candi Couture is printed on bodice of dress; rooted, long, black hair; brown painted eyes.
Marks: Hamilton Toys Inc, ©1990
Value: $40

Retro Bubble Cut Candi® (1998), *International Candi*® (2001), and *Retro Ponytail Candi*® (1998). All dolls have honey complexions. Retro dolls were marketed by Hamilton Design Systemé; *International Candi*® by Integrity Toys™. *Retro* dolls have honey hair color and green, painted eyes. *International Candi*® is a platinum blonde with a short, cropped afro; brown, painted eyes. All dolls wear original outfits.
Marks (all): Hamilton Toys, Inc. ©1990
Value: *Retro* dolls $35 each; *International Candi*® $75
Retro Charisse® by Mikelman (marked Integrity Toys™, below on left and right) and *Retro Candi*® by Hamilton™ with facial paint by Mikelman (middle doll), ca 1998. *Retro Charisse*® dolls have honey skin color, auburn hair, bubble cut (left) and ponytail (right). Middle doll is *Retro Candi*® with dark skin, pink lip color.
Charisse® **marks:** Integrity 1996; *Candi*® **marks:** Hamilton Design ©1990
Value: $35 each

Bebe Lollipop Girl® - Jan McLean Designs/Unimax Toys™, 2002; rooted green hair, large painted brown eyes; wears fuchsia dress with lime green boots with fuchsia fringe at top; very poseable. Box reads: "Inaugural Edition," sold through doll shops and doll dealers. Another less expensive version was sold through toy and department stores.
Value: $30

Boutique Fashion Doll®, Peggy-Ann Doll Clothes, Inc.™, ca. 1970s, vinyl head, thin plastic body, arms and legs; wears orange one-piece shorts with black belt; has brown, rooted hair styled in ponytail; painted, brown eyes, pink lip color. **Value:** $25

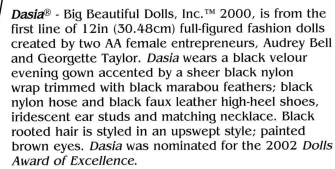

Dasia® - Big Beautiful Dolls, Inc.™ 2000, is from the first line of 12in (30.48cm) full-figured fashion dolls created by two AA female entrepreneurs, Audrey Bell and Georgette Taylor. *Dasia* wears a black velour evening gown accented by a sheer black nylon wrap trimmed with black marabou feathers; black nylon hose and black faux leather high-heel shoes, iridescent ear studs and matching necklace. Black rooted hair is styled in an upswept style; painted brown eyes. *Dasia* was nominated for the 2002 *Dolls Award of Excellence.*
Value: $75
Photograph courtesy of Georgette Taylor, Co-owner and VP, Big Beautiful Dolls, Inc.™

Destiny the Doctor® - Smartees, Inc.™, 1999; wears light green "scrubs," comes with stethoscope, first-aid kit, doctor's bag, comb, brush; official diploma, resumé, storybook, and glossary that teaches the meanings of the words in the storybook.
Value: $30

Fashion Fling Tariq® and *Fashion Fling Janay*® - Integrity Toys, Inc.™ 2001; *Tariq*®, 12in (30.48cm), honey complexion, shaven head; painted hazel eyes. *Janay*® is 11½in (29.21cm), honey complexion, light golden brown crimped hair that is rooted; painted, hazel eyes. Both wear tropical outfits.
Value: $20 each

G5 Vanessa® - the Get Set Club, Inc.™, 1999; wears yellow G-Five T-shirt, blue pants, blue and white sneakers, has extra yellow sports bra and shorts; G5 key ring included; has jointed wrists.
Value: $40

Imani Kente Fun® - Olmec Corp.™, 1991. Two versions - (Left) wears jumper made of Kente cloth print; (Right) has new *Imani*® face mold and wears Kente cloth print jacket, skirt, and hat. *Imani*® evolved from *Ellisse*®, who evolved from Olmec's first fashion doll, *Naomi*®. (see photo top of page 60.)
Value: $15 each

Maxi Mod® - Shillman™, ca. 1970s, vinyl head, thin plastic body, twist and turn waist. Doll on left is redressed. Doll on right wears yellow bathing suit. Both have bubble cut, rooted hairstyle; rooted lashes; painted brown eyes.
Value: $10 and $15 respectively

My Scene Madison® - Mattel™, 2002, 12in (30.48cm), comes with extra outfit, doll stand, sunglasses, purse.
Value: $20

Naomi® and *Ellisse*® - Olmec Corp.™, 1988 and 1989, respectively. First fashion doll by the Olmec Company. *Naomi*® was made one year only; company changed doll's name to *Ellisse*™ the second year. The same outfits were used for *Ellisse*™. Doll came in several different outfits and several different hairstyles in subsequent years before its name was changed to *Imani*®.
Value: $50 each

Grown Up Tammy® Ideal™ (Left to right) ca. 1963, ca. 1964 (box date); 12in (30.48cm), brown rooted hair, brown side-glancing eyes. (Right) Wears original red and white striped top, blue pleated mini-skirt; (Left) wears turquoise romper.
Value: (Left to right) $300 and $350
Doll on left courtesy of Michelle Hoskins; doll on right courtesy of Melodie Anderson

60

15½in (39.27cm) Fashion Dolls

Elle® - *Trendwatch Collector Series* - Jakks Pacific™, 2000 (Left); black rooted hair styled in a ponytail, painted brown eyes, closed mouth; wears original updated Western-style outfit; display stand. Several versions of *Elle®* were made wearing different outfits. The Black dolls sold out almost immediately and are still pursued by collectors today. Doll on right wears the Madame Alexander **Alex®** doll's outfit *Dinner and a Movie.*
Value: $50
Doll on right courtesy of Melodie Anderson

16in (40.64cm) Fashion Dolls

Daisy® of the "Somers and Field of London Collection" - Doug James and Laura Meisner for Knickerbocker™, 1999. Left to Right: *Picadilly, Trafalgar Square,* and *Milkmaid Wedding Daisy®.* Daisy Field® represents the 1960's Mod era. Dolls wear original outfits. Painted eyes with heavy eye makeup, closed mouths. *Picadilly Daisy®* has black rooted hair. The other two have brown rooted hair.
Marks: (Right buttocks) ™James and Meisner and the L.L. Knickerbocker Company, Inc. 1999. Various outfits were made for *Daisy®.*
Value: $100 each

Esme® - Robert Tonner, (Left to right) Basic *Esme*® (1999), ***Boston Bound Esme*®** (2001), LE 2000 and ***Cover Girl Esme*®** (2000), LE 3000. Basic *Esme*® is the debut version of the only Black doll in the *Tyler Wentworth® Collection.* Black rooted hair, brown painted eyes, closed mouth; jointed elbows and knees.

Marks: (Basic *Esme*® head) Robert Tonner Doll Co.™; same marks on back plus ©1999 All dolls wear their original outfits.

Value: (Left to right) $75, $125, and $150 *Boston Bound and Cover Girl Esme*® *courtesy of Melodie Anderson*

Esme® as **Tanza,** a one-of-a-kind (OOAK) by Marcia Cash was formerly a 16in (40.64cm) *Esme*® by Robert Tonner. *Tanza* has had a complete makeover. Her makeup has been completely repainted with artist quality acrylics for a fresh, natural look. The multitude of braided locks in her hair have been tipped with hundreds of seed beads in the colours of Mother Africa - red, gold, and green. She is playing with one of Traveler in Thyme's awesome 18in (45.72cm) beaded serpents.
Value: $400 (doll, wardrobe, snake)
Photo and description courtesy Marcia Cash, Traveler in Thyme
http://www.travelerinthyme.com

Esme® as *Uhura*, an OOAK by Marcia Cash was formerly a 16in (40.64cm) *Esme*® by Robert Tonner. *Uhura* has had a complete makeover to resemble a maiden of the Samburu tribe, a tribe of people known to dress their hair with mud. Her repaint was accomplished with natural earth pigments. A black, full-length, deerskin gown fits her curves perfectly. Her jewelry consists of bronzed coils. The incredible beadwork serpent is made from peyote stitch – over 6000 seeds and bugle beads in its 38in (96.52cm) length. Her beadwork snake can be removed to be worn as a necklace. The black leather gown is not removable.
Value: $475
Photo and description courtesy Marcia Cash, Traveler in Thyme http://www.travelerinthyme.com

Gone Gold Paris®, *LeConcorde Paris®*, and *Grand Entrance Paris®* - Madame Alexander™, 2001, wear original outfits, have brown, painted eyes; brunette wigs.
Values: $160, $100 and $200, respectively.
Photograph courtesy of Melodie Anderson

Violet Waters® "Special Appearance", the debut doll, by Mel Odom for ©Ashton Drake, the only Black doll in the *Gene Marshall*® Collection, 2001; represents a singer from the Billie Holiday era. Has brown rooted hair accented by white flower; painted eyes, open/closed mouth with painted teeth (appears to be singing); wears elaborate full-length, white gown embellished by hundreds of iridescent violet and white sequins and white faux pearls, faux pearl earrings, full-length white gloves, white stockings and ankle-strap shoes. Personalized doll stand and COA included.
Value: $150

18in (45.72cm) Fashion Dolls

SuperSize™ Christie® - Mattel™, 1976; has a soft vinyl face and a rigid vinyl body. Rooted brown, side-parted hair with auburn sun streaks that frame face; brown painted eyes; wears a pink satin and silver lamé body suit, matching full-length skirt, white shoes, faux diamond necklace and ring; has extra aqua outfit, aqua shoes, white doll stand.
Value: $200

Tiffany Taylor® - Ideal™, 1974; soft vinyl face, rigid vinyl body; Marks (head): 1973 CG 19H230 Hong Kong; (right buttocks) 1974 Ideal Hollis NY 11423 (Left) 2M-5854-01 1 Has long, rooted, auburn hair that turns black with a swivel of the skullcap. Heavy eye makeup with eyelashes, parted rust-colored lips. (Right) wears gold lamé body suit with lime green wrap, lime green mules; (Left) redressed in a 1970's Mego™ *Candy*® outfit.
Value: (Left to right) $75, $50

19in (48.26cm) ca. 1950's Fashion Dolls

1950's High-Heel Fashion Dolls high-heel feet; black, rooted hair styled in bubble cut; brown sleep eyes; closed mouths. (Left) wears bridal gown, veil, white high-heel shoes, pearl drop earrings. Marked "14R" on head. (Right) Wears pink, print halter-style dress, pearl drop earrings, slate blue high-heel shoes. Marked on head P.
Value: (Left to right) $65, $40

19in (48.26cm) *American Models Collection™* - **Robert Tonner.** Models have rooted, brunette hair and painted brown eyes.

Shonda® (1995) wears gray dress with Dalmatian trim, black pumps, LE 500
Value: $350

Carol® (1996) wears peach dress and silver sandals, LE 750 (production ran short)
Value: $200

Colette Bride® (1997) cream dress, cream shoes, LE 750
Value: $400 Other African-American dolls in the Robert Tonner *American Models Collection™* (not pictured) include: *Beverly Bride*® (1996 - VHTF), *Olivia*® (1998), and *Jasmine*® (1999)

Tonner Model photographs courtesy of Melodie Anderson

Ebony and Ivory Houndstooth Cissette®, ca. 1997; black wig; brown sleep eyes; closed mouth (black lip color); wears houndstooth suit, faux fur hat with netting, faux fur muffs, black stockings, black and white heels, snakeskin-like handbag.
Value: $125

Ebony and Ivory Houndstooth Cissy® (1996) LE under 50; VHTF; black hair and brown sleep eyes; wears houndstooth suit, matching hat with netting, black stockings, black and white shoes.
Value: $1000
Photograph courtesy of Valerie Myers

Hollywood Cissy® (2000) LE 1000; long, black hair; brown eyes; form-fitting, sleeveless brocade white gown adorned with shimmering sequins, faux white fur cape embroidered with swirled white appliqués, sequins and pearls, silver shoes.
Value: $500

Marc Bouwer Cissy® (1999) LE 500; black rooted hair; brown eyes; wears brown, full-length gold lamé gown with brown lining, brown feather stole, gold heels
Value: $500

(Left to right) *Tea Rose Cissy*® (1997) wears floral dress with floral hat, LE 50; *Cafe Rose Cissy*® (1996) wears white dress with matching faux fur-trimmed stole and matching hat, LE 50.
Value: $500 each
Photograph courtesy of Melodie Anderson

Other African American *Cissy*® dolls include *Barcelona Cissy*® (1998) LE 1000; *Collector's United Blue Danube*® (1999) LE under 50; *Collector's United Homecoming Queen*® (2000) LE under 50; *Society Stroll*® *(2000)* LE 500; *America the Beautiful*® (2001) LE 1500; *Alluring Amethyst*® (2002) LE 36; *Blue Bird*® LE 150 (2002).

Welcome to the world of imagination through doll play. Most of the dolls referenced in this chapter were manufactured as play dolls. Some dolls that were manufactured as collectible dolls are also included. Dolls referred to as "types" are those fashioned by one manufacturer after a popular doll that was originally made by a different manufacturer, i.e. *Playpal*-type.

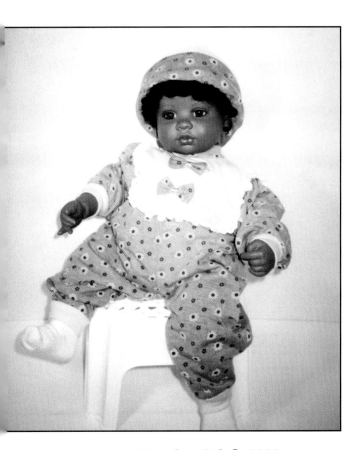

Adora Dolls™ - *Name Your Own Baby*®, 2001
Material: Vinyl head, hands, feet; stuffed, weighted-cloth arms and legs
Height: 19in (48.26cm)
Marks: (Head) KRV-047
Hair/Eyes/Mouth: Short, curly black wig/brown, stationary eyes with applied upper and lower eyelashes/open-closed mouth
Clothing: Lavender and pink romper with yellow flowers, matching hat, white socks
Value: $75

Allied Eastern (AE) Girl, ca. 1950's
Material: Vinyl
Height: 11½in (29.21cm)
Hair/Eyes/Mouth: Molded hair styled in a bun/brown, sleep eyes with painted upper and lower eyelashes/closed mouth
Clothing: Redressed in peach and white gingham dress, white panties, white socks and shoes over molded socks and shoes
Value: $40

Allied Eastern (AE), *Playpal*-type ca. 1958
Material: Soft vinyl face; rigid vinyl body, arms, and legs
Height: 36in (91.44cm)
Marks: (Head) AE3651 #31
Hair/Eyes/Mouth: Rooted, black hair/brown, sleep eyes/closed mouth
Clothing: Redressed in a vintage 50's style dress, white socks and shoes
Value: $250
Photograph courtesy of Mrs. Josie Henry

Madame Alexander™ - *Memories of a Lifetime*® for McDonalds™ *Bride, Groom, Cool Cathy*, 2002
Material: rigid vinyl with jointed arms, legs, heads
Height: 5in (12.7cm)
Hair/Eyes/Mouth: *Bride* and *Cool Cathy* have glued on ponytails. *Groom*'s hair is molded/all have brown sleep eyes/closed mouths
Clothing: *Groom* wears black tux with molded-on black pants. *Bride* wears white satin gown with veil, molded hat. *Cool Cathy* wears painted-on fuchsia T-shirt with yellow star, molded denim jeans.
Other: Promotional dolls sold at McDonald's or included in their Happy Meals
Value: $5 each

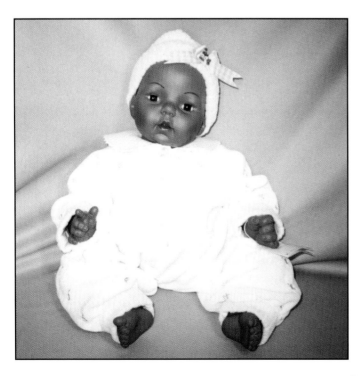

Madame Alexander™ - *Lifelike Baby Victoria*®, 1998
Material: Vinyl with stuffed, weighted-cloth body
Height: 19in (48.26cm)
Marks: (Head) ©Alexander 1966
Hair/Eyes/Mouth: Black, molded hair/brown, sleep eyes
Clothing: White velour romper with embroidered pink roses, pink and white checkered collar, white cap with pink and white checkered bow
Other: This is a reproduction of the original (Caucasian-only), 1966 Baby Victoria. The African American doll was introduced in 1998.
Value: $100

American Classic - *Lottie*, ca. 1990's
Material: Porcelain head, arms, legs; stuffed-cloth body
Height: 19in (48.26cm)
Hair/Eyes/Mouth: Long, black wig/hazel, stationary eyes/closed mouth
Clothing: All original cream and pink Victorian-style dress with matching hat
Other: Doll is named for the collector's daughter
Value: $75
Photograph courtesy of Unistine Harris

Avon™ *Tender Memories Collection Batter Up*® and *Girl Scout*®, 1995
Material: Vinyl head, hands, feet; stuffed-cloth body, arms and upper legs
Height: 19in (48.26cm)
Hair/Eyes/Mouth: Black wigs/brown stationary eyes/closed mouths
Clothing: *Girl Scout* (GS) wears GS uniform with box of GS cookies. *Batter Up* wears baseball uniform, cap, black vinyl sneakers, and holds a wooden bat
Value: $40 each

Ashle Belle™ - **Connie**® and **Danny**®, ca. 2000
Material: Porcelain heads, breastplates, arms, legs; cloth bodies
Height: 19in (48.26cm)
Hair/Eyes/Mouth: Gray wigs/brown, stationary eyes/closed mouths
Value: $20 each
Photograph courtesy of Ruth Joyner

Berjusa™ - **Angel Face**®, ca. 1992
Material: All vinyl with jointed arms and legs
Height: 13in (33.02cm)
Marks: (Head) ©Berjusa
Hair/Eyes/Mouth: Rooted, long, curly hair/brown, stationary eyes/puckered lips
Clothing: Multicolored shirt with matching shorts, matching headband, yellow socks, white vinyl lace-up sneakers
Value: $50
Photograph courtesy of Angela Garrett Terry

Checkerboard Toys™ - **Dale**® and **Fab Fashion Fun Denise**® 2001
Material: All vinyl
Height: 6½in (16.51cm)
Hair/Eyes/Mouth: *Dale*: Rooted bubble cut. *Denise*: Rooted, long, straight black hair/both have painted eyes/closed mouths.
Clothing: *Dale* wears orange knit dress, bronze pumps. *Denise:* Fuchsia top, fuchsia and gold brocade skit, fuchsia boots, comes with extra outfit.
Other: *Dale* is a reproduction of the 1970s doll. *Denise* was not available on the market until 2002.
Value: $35 each

Cabbage Patch Talking Kids® (CPK), 1987
Material: Vinyl head; soft-sculptured body, arms, hands, and feet
Height: 18in (45.72cm)
Marks: Green signature on buttocks: Xavier Roberts. (Head) T8/©1978, 1983, O.A.A., Inc. (Body tag) ©1987Cabbage Patch Kids, Original Appalachian Art Works, Inc./P (for patent) ©1987 Original Appalachian Art Works, Inc
Hair/Eyes/Mouth: Dark brown, rooted hair/painted, brown eyes/open mouth
Clothing: all original outfit
Other: Doll's mouth moves when she talks. Comes with cup that programs the voice. Two talking CPK dolls can interact with each other.
Value: $150

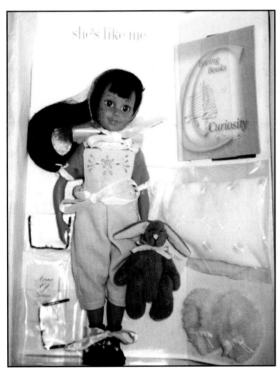

The Family Company™ - **She's Like Me Madison®** *"Loving Books,"* 1999
Material: Rigid vinyl
Height: 9in (22.86cm)
Marks: (Back) ©1999 The Family Company
Hair/Eyes/Mouth: Long, brown, straight wig with bangs/brown, stationary eyes/closed mouth
Clothing: Original outfit; holds brown stuffed rabbit; has two pairs of reading glasses, white eyelet pillow, pink furry slippers
Other: Mini book: *Loving Books Curiosity;* mock book: *Anne of Green Gables*
Value: $45

EG/E. Goldberger™ - **Walking Annette®**, ca. 1970s
Material: Rigid vinyl
Height: 32in (81.28cm)
Hair/Eyes/Mouth: Rooted afro/brown sleep eyes/closed mouth
Clothing: Granny-style dress with solid red bodice and ruffled hem with multicolored print skirt, white socks; black, vinyl shoes
Other: Comes with hairstyling set
Value: $150

Fun World, Inc.™ - *Soul Sister*®, ca. 1970
Material: Vinyl
Height: 8in (20.32cm)
Hair/Eyes/Mouth: Rooted, black curly hair/painted, oversized eyes/closed mouth
Clothing: Original outfits
Value: $25 each

Furga™ - *Florence*®, ca. 1993
Material: Vinyl with stuffed cloth body, upper arms and legs
Height: 31in (78.74cm)
Marks: (Head) 1/Furga Dolls logo/478
Hair/Eyes/Mouth: Rooted, curly ponytail with bangs/brown, stationary eyes applied upper eyelashes/closed mouth
Clothing: Original outfit
Value: $200

Georgetown Dolls™ and L. L. Knickerbocker™ - *Magic Attic Club Keisha*®, L - R: ca. 1996 and 1995
Material: All vinyl
Height: 18in (45.72cm)
Hair/Eyes/Mouth: Brown, kanekalon wig/brown, stationary eyes/closed mouths
Clothing: All original
Other: Doll mold by Robert Tonner. The first Magic Attic Club (MAC) dolls originally manufactured by Georgetown Dolls™ in 1994 did not include *Keisha*®. *Keisha*® was added to the line in 1995 (the doll on the right). Georgetown Dolls™ sold the MAC line to L.L. Knickerbocker™ in 1996. *Keisha*® and the other MAC dolls were given new outfits (the doll on the left). *Keisha*® comes with a book. Several different outfits and accessories sold separately. Paper dolls were also sold separately (see Paper Dolls chapter). At time of publication, the MAC line is owned by Marian LLC.
Value: $80 each
Photograph courtesy of Debra Richardson

Gotz™ - *Mein Baby*® - *My Baby*® - *Mon Bébé*®, ca. 1985, West Germany
Material: Vinyl, brown cloth body
Height: 21in (53.34cm)
Marks: (Head) Götz Puppe
Hair/Eyes/Mouth: Molded hair/brown, sleep eyes/open-closed mouth
Clothing: Original outfit with "Götz Modell" logo pinned to blouse. White eyelet bonnet may or may not be original to doll.
Value: $75

Hasbro/Ibot 2000™ - *My Real Baby*™, 2000
Material: Vinyl head, lower arms and feet, cloth body
Height: 21in (53.34cm)
Hair/Eyes/Mouth: Black, rooted hair/brown, stationary eyes/smiling mouth that moves when interacting
Clothing: Original clothing
Other: Requires six AA batteries to interact through facial expressions and realistic emotional responses; speech develops over time.
Value: $150

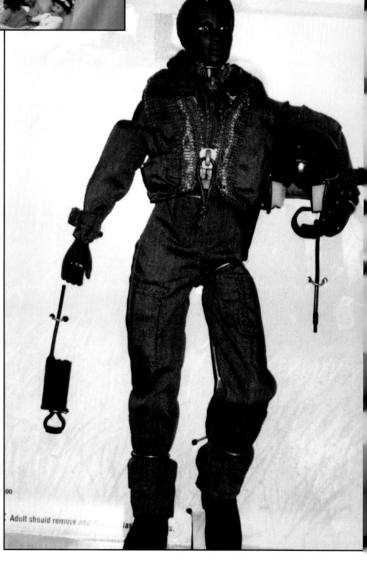

Hasbro™ - *LE Classic Collection GI Jane US Army Helicopter Pilot*®, 1997
Material: Vinyl, jointed
Height: 11in (27.94cm)
Hair/Eyes/Mouth: Black, molded hair/painted eyes/closed mouth
Clothing: Original, military-style
Other: First female doll in the *GI Joe*® line
Value: $75
Photograph courtesy of Freda Goldston

Herman Pecker Dolls, ca. late 1960's
Material: Soft vinyl/rubber heads, plastic bodies
Height: 9in (22.86cm)
Marks: (Body) Made in Hong Kong
Hair/Eyes/Mouth: Rooted, black hair/painted, side-glancing, black eyes/closed mouths
Clothing: Right doll wears pink striped pajamas with matching nightcap. Original tag reads: "#1418 Made Exclusively for Herman Pecker & Co., Inc." Left wears a white, satin-like dress trimmed with lace; white ribbon in hair, white underwear.
Value: $20 each
Photograph courtesy of Bonnie Lewis

Horsman™ - *Thirstee Walker*®, ca 1964
Material: Soft-vinyl face, rigid-vinyl body, arms, and legs
Height: 27in (68.58cm)
Marks: (Head) Horsman Dolls© Inc./19©64 TB26 (Back) Made in China
Hair/Eyes/Mouth: Brown, rooted hair styled in two loose ponytails/brown, sleep eyes/open mouth
Clothing: Original red and white flannel pajamas, replaced bottle
Value: $100

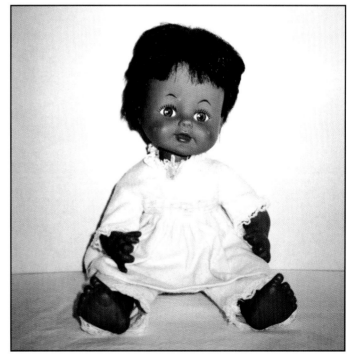

Horsman™ - **Unknown Musical Baby**, ca. 1967
Material: Soft vinyl
Height: 12in (30.48cm)
Marks: (Head) 13/Horsman Dolls, Inc./1967 (Lower Back) 30
Hair/Eyes/Mouth: Brown, rooted hair/brown, stationary eyes/drinker mouth
Clothing: Pink flannel top and pants
Other: Doll has pull string in back that activates music box (Brahms Lullaby) and causes head to move from side to side
Value: $45

Ideal™ - *Giggles*™, 1968
Material: Soft-vinyl head, rigid-vinyl body, arms, legs
Height: 18in (45.72cm)
Marks: (Head) 1966 Ideal Toy Corp. GG-18-H-77 (Buttocks) ©1967 Ideal Toy Corp. GG-18
Hair/Eyes/Mouth: Brown, rooted hair/brown, googly eyes/open smiling mouth
Clothing: Lime, yellow, orange, pink striped top; matching shorts, black sandals
Other: Doll's head and eyes move from side to side when her arms are outstretched and brought together or separated, which causes her to giggle
Value: $350

Jessie Collection™ (Canada) 1990 and 1995 Girl Dolls
Material: Vinyl head, arms, legs; stuffed cloth body
Height: 26in (66.04cm)
Marks: Tag sewn to backs of both dolls: Certificate of Originality Jessie Collection™ This doll is an original artistic Jessie Collection™ designed especially for the most serious collector. Series 1990 (1990 doll); Series 1995 (1995) doll. Importations Jacques Fournier LTD, St.-Georges Beauce (Québec) Canada G5Y 5CA.
Hair/Eyes/Mouth: Black, curly rooted hair/brown, sleep eyes/open-closed mouths
Clothing: The 1990 doll wears original outfit with Jessie Collection™ metal logo pinned to romper. The 1995 doll is redressed in a size 18-month child's dress, red patent-leather shoes. Original dress is orange, blue and white print with metal Jessie Collection™ pin logo.
Value: $60 each

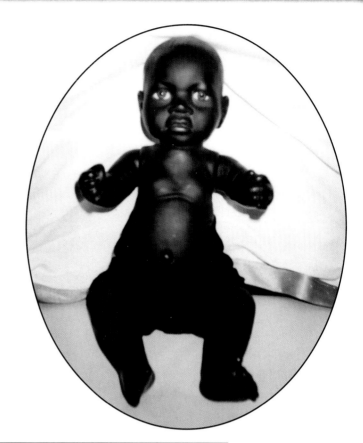

Karda Products™, Australia - Australia Boy, 1998
Material: Ebony colored vinyl
Marks: (Head) ©Karda 1998
Height: 18in (45.72cm)
Hair/Eyes/Mouth: Molded brown hair/brown, stationary eyes/closed mouth
Clothing: Wears black cloth as diaper. Original diaper was red.
Value: $60
Photograph courtesy of Sharon Margaret Rainey

Karda Products™, Australia - Australian Aboriginal Boy and Girl Child Dolls, 1994
Material: Ebony colored vinyl
Marks: (Head) Karda Products Australia ©1994
Height: 17in (43.18cm)
Hair/Eyes/Mouth: Rooted, medium brown hair with reddish brown highlights/medium-brown, glass, sleep eyes/closed mouth
Clothing: (Boy) red cotton shorts; red string tied around head; (Girl) cotton sleeveless, pale green dress with white tribal designs; two feathers in hair, black cotton panties
Other: White painted tribal marks on boy's cheeks, upper arms and torso; broad facial features
Value: $75 each
Photograph courtesy of Bonnie Lewis

Keisha Dolls™ - *Keisha*, ca. 1983
Material: All soft vinyl
Height: 23in (58.42cm)
Marks: (Head) Keisha II/©H.J.S. 1983/008695
Hair/Eyes/Mouth: Rooted, long black hair with crimped ponytail hairpiece/brown sleep eyes/closed mouth
Clothing: Gold lamé sleeveless one-piece jumper, gold lamé sandals, wears Nefertiti necklace and earrings made by the owner
Other: Doll may represent Nefertiti
Value: $75

Top right: Keisha Dolls™ - (Left to right) *Ronnie*®, *Keisha*®, and *Makeda*®, 1983-1991
Material: All soft vinyl
Height: 23in (58.42cm)
Marks: (Head) Keisha II/©H.J.S. 1983/008695
Hair/Eyes/Mouth: Rooted, black hair. The doll on the far right also has a hairpiece attached to the top of her head.
Clothing: All original outfits
Value: $75 each
Photograph courtesy of Debra Richardson

Kenner™ - *The Baby-Sitter's Club Jessi*®, 1993
Material: Vinyl
Height: 19in (48.26cm)
Hair/Eyes/Mouth: Long, black rooted hair/brown, painted eyes/smiling mouth with painted teeth
Clothing: All original
Other: VHTF, comes with mini book, *The Baby-Sitter's Club* starring Jessi (Jessica) Ramsey, by Ann M. Martin, Scholastic Books
Value: $100

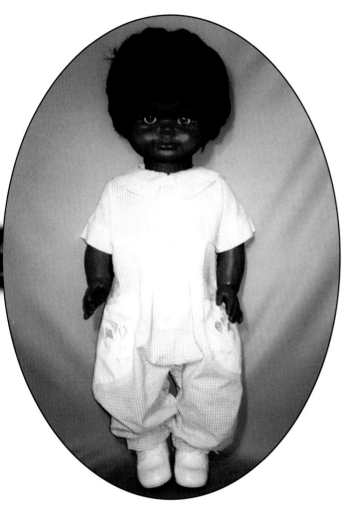

Mattel™ - *Baby Brother Tender Love*®, 1975
Material: All vinyl, jointed arms, non-jointed legs
Height: 13in (33.02cm)
Marks: (Head) ©1972 Mattel Inc. (Body) ©1975 Mattel Inc. USA
Hair/Eyes/Mouth: Rooted, brown hair/brown, painted eyes/drinker mouth
Clothing: Aqua, yellow and white striped shirt, aqua short pants
Other: Doll is anatomically correct, drinks from mouth, wets in diaper
Value: $65

Lissi (Batz) Company™, W. Germany-**Unknown Girl** ca. 1970s (made before the unification of Germany).
Material: All vinyl with bent baby legs
Height: 26in (66.04cm)
Marks: (Head) LB in triangle 70/2C
Hair/Eyes/Mouth: Short, black, rooted hair/brown sleep eyes with black eyelashes/closed mouth
Clothing: Redressed in infant's romper, white socks, white leather baby shoes
Value: $200

Mattel™ - *Baby-Skates*®, 1982
Material: Soft-vinyl head and arms, rigid-plastic body and legs
Height: 15in (38.1cm)
Marks: (Head) 36 © Mattel, Inc. 1980
Hair/Eyes/Mouth: Brown, rooted hair/brown, side-glancing sleep eyes/open-closed smiling mouth
Clothing: Yellow and pink striped top, pink jogging pants, yellow elbow and knee pads, athletic shoe roller skates
Other: Mattel's first, wind-up skating doll
Value: $75

Mego™ - **Nubia**®, 1976
Material: All vinyl
Height: 12in (30.48cm)
Marks: (Head) ©DC COMICS/INC 1976
Hair/Eyes/Mouth: Black, rooted hair with silver streak on right/painted eyes/closed mouth
Clothing: All original
Other: Nubia® is Wonder Woman's nemesis
Value: $150
Photograph courtesy of Michelle Hoskins

Lee Middleton Original Dolls™ - **Playtime Wonder**® (PTW) and **Small Wonder**® (SW), 2001 and 1998 (play line dolls)
Material: Vinyl heads, arms, and legs; stuffed-cloth body
Height: 19in (48.26cm); 18in (45.72cm)
Marks: (PTW, head) 2000 Lee Middleton Original Dolls by Reva; (SW head) 1998 Lee Middleton Original Dolls by Reva
Hair/Eyes/Mouth: (PTW) brunette, long, rooted hair originally hung loose, restyled in two ponytails/brown, stationary eyes with applied eyelashes/open mouth with molded tongue, two upper teeth. (SW) brunette, rooted hair/brown, stationary eyes with applied eyelashes/closed mouth
Clothing: (PTW) Dressed in Lee Middleton Original™ aqua dress. Original outfit - pink satin dress, came with extra outfit of burgundy sweatshirt with khaki skirt, burgundy shoes. (SW) Original pink gown and hat.
Value: $60 each

Munecas bb™ - **My Baby**®, ca. 1980s
Material: Vinyl with stuffed-cloth body
Height: 18in (45.72cm)
Marks: (Head) bb
Hair/Eyes/Mouth: Black, rooted hair/brown, sleep eyes/open-closed mouth
Clothing: Original clothing
Value: $35
Photograph courtesy of Karen Kilburn

My Twinn® - 2002
Material: Vinyl head, lower arms and legs; stuffed-cloth body, upper arms and legs with armature and multiple joints for posing
Height: 24in (60.96cm)
Marks: (Head) My Twinn, Inc.® 1997
Hair/Eyes/Mouth: Black, straight wig styled by collector in two ponytails and given bangs/brown stationary eyes with applied upper and lower eyelashes/smiling, closed mouth
Clothing: *My Twinn®* Pink Poodle outfit — white blouse, pink fleece poodle skirt, black patent-leather belt, white bobby socks, black and white saddle oxfords, two silk scarves used for hair accents (one is supposed to be for doll's neck)
Other: The *My Twinn®* dolls are made-to-order to look like photographs submitted to the company. Each doll is individually crafted. No two dolls are alike. This doll was purchased from another collector.
Value: $200

Playmates Toys, Inc.™ -
Amazing Ally®, 1999 – 2001
Material: Soft vinyl face, rigid vinyl body
Height: 18in (45.72cm)
Marks: Instructions for use printed on body
Hair/Eyes/Mouth: Brunette, rooted hair/brown eyes/open mouth that moves when she speaks
Clothing: All original
Other: Winner of 1999 *Parents* Award; doll on right is *Amazing Ally with Kitty®*
Value: $75
Photograph courtesy of Debra Richardson

Playskool™ - *Baby Dolly Surprise*®, 1988
Material: Jointed vinyl
Height: 14in (35.56cm)
Marks: (Head) 1986 Playskool Inc. (Body) US Patent number (unreadable), Made in China
Hair/Eyes/Mouth: Rooted, brown hair with center ponytail that grows when right arm is raised/brown, painted eyes/closed mouth
Clothing: Multicolored pastel romper, comb and brush included
Other: Young Raven Symone (*The Cosby Show*) is pictured on doll's box holding doll
Value: $50

Pleasant Company™ and Pleasant Company Publications™ - *American Girl Addy*® (1993), *Mini Addy*® and book (1995), *Addy Paper Doll*® (1994).
Material: Vinyl and cloth (larger and mini dolls); paper (paper doll)
Height: Larger doll 18in (45.72cm); mini doll 5in (12.7cm); paper doll 10in (25.4cm)
Marks: (Head, larger doll) Pleasant Company 148/15
Hair/Eyes/Mouth: Kanekalon wig/brown, stationary eyes/open-closed mouth with two upper teeth
Clothing: All original
Value: $100 (larger doll), $25 (mini doll and book), $15 paper doll
Larger doll courtesy of Angela Garrett Terry

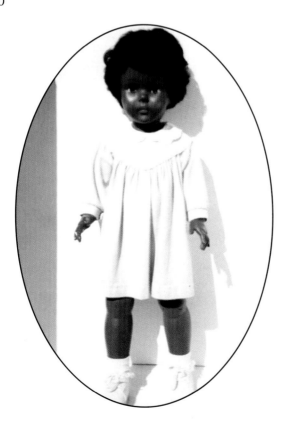

Reliable Toys™ - *Companion Doll*®, ca. 1970's
Material: Rubber face; vinyl body, arms and legs
Height: 30in (76.2cm)
Marks: (Head) Reliable Toys Made in Canada
Hair/Eyes/Mouth: Black, curly, rooted hair/brown, sleep eyes with lashes/closed mouth
Clothing: Redressed
Value: $100

Remco Industries™ - *Singing Mimi*®, 1973.
Material: All vinyl
Height: 20in (50.8cm)
Marks: (Head) 12/Remco Inc. 19 ©73 (back) Sound Device Made in Japan (Above buttocks) ©1973 Remco IND. INC
Hair/Eyes/Mouth: Black, rooted hair/brown, painted eyes/closed mouth
Clothing: Red blouse, purple mini skirt and tights, black shoes, purple tam; not wearing purple jacket
Other: Sings "I'd like to Teach the World to Sing" and other songs in 8 languages — English, French, German, Greek, Polish, Hebrew, Spanish, and Italian. Tiny records placed in her back activate her singing mechanism.
Value: $100
Photograph courtesy of Michelle Hoskins

Royal™ - *Tammy Candy Striper*® doll, made in Canada, 1961
Material: All vinyl
Height: 10½in (26.67cm)
Marks: (Head) Royal Doll
Hair/Eyes/Mouth: Black, rooted hair styled in two ponytails/brown sleep eyes/closed mouth
Clothing: Pink and white Candy Striper dress, white pantaloons, black shoes, hangtag
Value: $45
Photograph courtesy of Linda C. Hayes

Unmarked, 1960's dolls and *Tammy*® by Royal™.
Material: All vinyl
Height: Far left and far right: 10½in (26.67cm), middle doll 19in (48.26cm)
Hair/Eyes/Mouth: Smaller dolls have black rooted hair, larger has brown rooted hair/all have brown sleep eyes/closed mouths
Clothing: Larger doll is redressed; all wear replaced white shoes
Value: $25, $50 and $35 respectively

In 1980, when the played-with *Little Soft Janie®*, opposite page, was purchased new, the author was so intrigued by the doll's true-to-life facial features, that she launched an investigation into the doll's origin. That investigation led to a desire for more of the company's delightful dolls for her daughter. Some 30 years later, the author is still intrigued by Shindana™ dolls and the history of Shindana Toys, Inc.™. The author is particularly awe-inspired by one of the company's co-founders, the late, Mr. Louis S. Smith, Jr. He and his cofounder, Mr. Robert Hall, worked diligently and successfully to provide the doll community with the first mass-produced Black dolls that looked like real Black people.

In this author's book, Mr. Smith and Mr. Hall will remain legendary doll-manufacturing heroes for time immemorial. The legacy of Shindana Toys, Inc.™ will forever live through the delightful and highly sought-after dolls and toys manufactured under their leadership. Their dolls are truly "Dolls Made by a Dream."

Shindana's Toys, Inc.™ a Division of Operation Bootstrap
(Company Highlights)

- The company was founded in an effort to rebuild the Watts (Los Angeles) community after the 1965 Watts riots.
- Shindana Toys, Inc.™ is the first company in the United States to mass-produce Black dolls with true-to-life facial features.
- Shindana Toys, Inc.™ was black-owned and operated. The company received funding and other aid from Mattel™, but maintained total control of operations.
- While the name, Shindana means "to compete" in the Swahili language, Shindana Toys, Inc.™ never marketed toys that promoted violence.
- The company's dolls, games, and other playthings promoted self-pride and self-esteem through the creation of dolls that looked like real Black people. Their dolls were not just white dolls "colored" brown.
- Many of the dolls were given Swahili names, the meanings of which were defined on the dolls' boxes or accompanying literature.
- Shindana Toys, Inc.™ celebrated the accomplishments of African-American personalities by creating dolls in their likeness.
- Shindana Toys, Inc.™ dolls and toys promoted career aspirations for children.
- Shindana Toys, Inc.™ promoted Black history awareness via Black history games and trivia.
- The company's motto was: "Dolls Made by a Dream."

Shindana Toys, Inc.™ Doll Marks: Shindana Toys, Inc.™ manufactured hundreds of dolls. All of the dolls are marked Shindana and/or Operation Bootstrap on their necks and/or backs along with the year of manufacture. For the NRFB dolls in this chapter, the marks are not included in their description.

Baby Nancy® - very first doll by Shindana Toys, Inc.™
Height: 13in (33.02cm)
Marks: Four versions of this doll were made. Two dolls were introduced in 1968 (pictured on left and in center), stock #2002 - ponytail and #2003 - afro. In 1969, a new *Baby Nancy* face mold was introduced (pictured on far right). There were two versions of that mold - stock #2002 for 1969 (ponytail), stock #2003 for 1969 (short curly hair).
Hair/Eyes/Mouth: All dolls have rooted hair/painted eyes/drinker mouth. The 1968 dolls have two painted upper teeth and one painted lower tooth. The 1969 dolls do not have teeth.
Value: 1968 $60; 1969 $40

Little Soft Janie®, 1975
Material: vinyl
Height: 9½in (24.13cm)
Marks: (Head) Shindana Toys ©1975 Made in Hong Kong
Hair/Eyes/Mouth: Black rooted hair originally styled in two pigtails/painted, brown eyes/closed mouth
Value: Played with doll $10; MIB doll $25
Doll on left courtesy of Angela Garrett Terry

Baby Zuri®, 1972
Material: Soft vinyl
Height: 13in (33.02cm)
Hair/Eyes/Mouth: Molded hair/painted brown eyes/closed mouth
Clothing: Original outfit
Other: *Baby Zuri*® is a girl, often mistaken for a boy. Zuri means beautiful in Swahili. This is the dark vinyl version. A lighter vinyl version was also made.
Value: $50

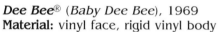

Dee Bee® (*Baby Dee Bee*), 1969
Material: vinyl face, rigid vinyl body
Height: 13in (33.02cm)
Hair/Eyes/Mouth: Rooted, straight black hair/painted, brown eyes/open-closed mouth
Clothing: Leopard-print romper
Value: $50

Dreamy Walker®, 1975
Material: Rubber face, vinyl body, arms and legs
Height: 32in (81.28cm)
Hair/Eyes/Mouth: Black, rooted hair in "shag" style/brown, sleep eyes/closed mouth
Clothing: Redressed in size 2T child's dress, white tights, black patent-leather shoes; (original outfit - bright red blouse with light blue overalls)
Value: $100

Disco Wanda®, 1978
Material: Soft-vinyl face, rigid-vinyl body
Height: 11½in (29.21cm)
Hair/Eyes/Mouth: Rooted, black hair/painted, brown eyes/open-closed smiling mouth, painted teeth
Clothing: Different disco-style outfits/extra outfit included in the box
Value: $35 each

Kim Jeans 'N Things®, 1972
Material: Soft vinyl face, rigid-vinyl body
Height: 15in (38.1cm)
Hair/Eyes/Mouth: Rooted, black hair/brown, painted eyes/closed mouth
Clothing: Original denim outfit. Extra outfit: Floral blouse and scarf, full-length, light blue, denim skirt with matching floral trim
Value: $35

Kim Jeans 'N Things®, ca 1970s
Different face mold, dolls wear three different outfits made for *Kim Jeans 'N Things*®.

Li'l Souls Family™: *Coochy*®, *Wilky*®, *Sis*®, 1971 and *Jo Jo*®, 1972.
Material: Cloth and yarn for hair
Height: (Left to right) 6½in, 10½in, 9½in and 16in (16.51cm, 26.67cm, 24.13cm, 40.64cm)
Marks: Body tags with Shindana Toys, Inc. ©1970 (*Coochy*, *Wilky*, or *Sis*); Jo Jo's body tag is dated ©1972
Hair/Eyes/Mouth: Huge afro hairstyles made with yarn/screen-printed eyes, cheeks and mouths
Clothing: *Silky*® and *Sis*® wear T-shirts with positive slogans such as "Learn Baby Learn," "Say it Loud," "Peace," and "Right on." *Coochy*® wears a pink, sewn-on romper with attached white bib with the letter C on it.
Other: Dolls came with *Little Souls Family*™ coloring book. *Natra*® (not pictured) was also a member of the *Little Souls Family*™ and larger versions of *Wilky*® and *Sis*® with different clothing and faces were made in approximately 1974.

Little Karee® and *Baby Kimmie*®, 1975, 1973
Material: Soft-vinyl faces, rigid vinyl bodies
Height: 9½in (24.13cm); 12in (30.48cm)
Hair/Eyes/Mouth: Black, rooted hair/brown, sleep eyes/drinker mouth
Clothing: Original clothing
Value: $25 each

Little Friends Collection™
Boy and Girl, 1976
Material: Soft vinyl, jointed arms and legs, movable head
Height: 12in (30.48cm)
Hair/Eyes/Mouth: (Boy) - molded hair; (Girl) - black rooted styled in two ponytails/painted eyes/drinker mouth
Clothing: Original outfits
Other: The *Little Friends Collection™* are representative of different ethnicities. There were also girls and boys representing Caucasian, Hispanic, Asian, and Native American children.
Value: $45

Malaika®, 1969
Material: Soft vinyl face, rigid-vinyl body
Height: 15in (38.1cm)
Hair/Eyes/Mouth: Rooted afro/painted, brown eyes/closed mouth
Clothing: Original outfit. Box indicates "Exclusive Afro American Fashions by Aajib"
Value: $50

Slade Super Agent®, 1975
Material: Vinyl, painted
Height: 9½in (24.13cm)
Hair/Eyes/Mouth: Molded afro/brown, painted eyes/ mustache, closed mouth
Clothing: Faux leather jacket, pants, orange shirt, carries briefcase with super agent gadgets
Value: $150

Talking Tamu®, 1970
Material: Vinyl head and hands; stuffed-cloth body, arms, legs, and feet
Height: 16in (40.64cm)
Hair/Eyes/Mouth: Rooted, black afro/ painted, brown eyes/closed mouth
Clothing: Original clothing
Other: Tamu means "sweet" in Swahili. Talking Tamu is a pull-string talker and says 18 "sweet" phrases, such as "Pick me up," and "Hold me tight"
Value: $150

Wanda the Career Girl, 1972-1975 (preceded *Disco Wanda*)
Material: All vinyl with jointed arms and legs, bendable knees
Height: 9in (22.86cm)
Marks: (lower back) 1972 Shindana Toys/Made in Hong Kong
Hair/Eyes/Mouth: Rooted, black hair/painted, brown eyes, rooted eyelashes/open-closed mouth with painted teeth
Value: *Wanda the Career Girl Parachuter/Race Car Driver* $50; *Professional Singer* $75; *Professional Tennis Player* $75. The loose doll is the original *Wanda the Career Girl* wearing a lime green micro mini dress and green heels $75 (loose) $100 NRFB.
Value: *Wanda the Career Girl Stewardess* $100; *Ballerina* $75

Wanda the Career Girl Nurse
Value: $75 (loose) $150 NRFB

94

Takara Toys™ - *Black Licca*®, 2000, part of the *Jenny* line, 9½in (24.13cm), made and sold only in Japan.
Value: $75

Tomy™ - *Kimberly*®, aka *Kimberly Cheerleader*, 1983
Material: All vinyl
Height: 17in (43.18cm)
Hair/Eyes/Mouth: Long black, rooted hair/painted, brown eyes/closed mouth
Clothing: White "Kimberly" top, red cheerleader skirt, white socks, red and white vinyl sneakers, cardboard megaphone, pompons, and pendant included
Value: $85
Photograph courtesy of Melodie Anderson

Roller Skating Kimberly® and other *Kimberly*® dolls: (Left to right) *Roller Skating Kimberly*®, *Kimberly*® wearing ice skating, soccer, jogging and school special occasion outfits. Many of *Kimberly*® doll's outfits were made by Cinderella® and Hang Ten®.
Photograph courtesy of Melodie Anderson

Robert Tonner Doll Company™ - **Penny and Friends**®, 2000
Material: All vinyl
Height: 19in (48.26cm)
Marks: (Head) "Penny"/©2000 Robert Tonner Doll Co.
Hair/Eyes/Mouth: Long, black straight wig with bangs/brown, stationary eyes/closed mouth
Clothing: Gold-rimmed eye glasses, white T-shirt; red faux leather zipper vest and skirt; black, faux leather, knee-high boots
Other: Sold exclusively through JCPenney stores
Value: $75

Topper™ - **Baby Catch-A-Ball**®, 1969
Material: Rigid vinyl, jointed arms and legs
Height: 18in (45.72cm)
Marks: (Head) Deluxe Topper 1968
Hair/Eyes/Mouth: Short, black curly rooted hair/brown stationary eyes with eyelashes/open/closed mouth with molded tongue stuck out to side
Clothing: wears original outfit
Other: Battery-operated, catches ball and throws it back
Value: $150

Topper™ - **Dale**®, **Van**®, **Dale**®, 1970
Material: Vinyl
Height: 6½in (16.51cm)
Hair/Eyes/Mouth: Dale® has rooted hair; boyfriend, Van®, has molded hair/all have painted eyes/closed mouths
Clothing: (Left to right): (Dale) Silver lamé and pink nylon gown, white shoes; (Van) football uniform; (Dale) multicolored top, green jumpsuit, turquoise shoes
Other: Dolls are from the 1970s Dawn® line
Value: $40 each

Wright Toys, Inc.™ - *Christine*®, ca. late 1960's
Material: Made of Lyka, a new type of vinyl with jointed arms and legs
Height: 19in (48.26cm)
Marks: (Head) 11/B. Wright
Hair/Eyes/Mouth: Rooted, black hair styled in two braids/brown, sleep eyes/open/closed mouth
Clothing: White dress with blue and yellow rickrack trim at bodice and hem
Other: Beatrice Wright was an African-American entrepreneur who manufactured Black dolls with true-to-life ethnic features. The same mold was used for most of her Black dolls. The molds were later sold to Totsy™, ca 1980's, who used their name on the dolls they produced.
Value: $75

Uneeda™ - *Playpal*-Type Companion Doll and DE-marked *Playpal*- Type Companion doll, ca. 1960's
Material: Both: All vinyl (soft vinyl face, rigid vinyl body), with metal walking mechanism that allows doll to walk with child when doll's left hand is held
Height: 36in (91.44cm)
Marks: (Left to right) (Heads) U5 and DE32
Hair/Eyes/Mouth: (Left) Black, short curly rooted/brown sleep eyes/closed mouth; (Right) black long, straight rooted hair with bangs/brown sleep eyes with black eyelashes/closed mouth
Clothing: (Left) Original pink dress, white panties, socks, shoes; (Right) redressed in child's 2T floral dress; original, pink shoes
Value: $250 and $200 respectively

97

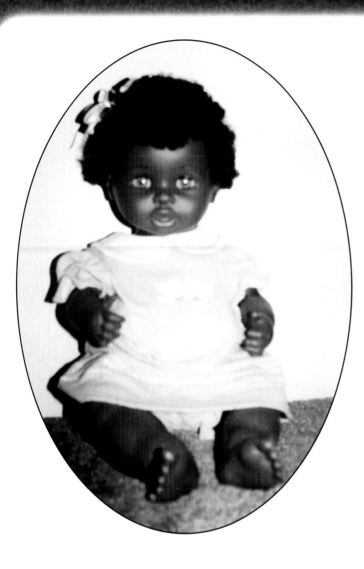

VICMA™ - *Ella*®, ca. 1980's
Material: rigid vinyl
Height: 22in (55.88cm)
Marks: (Head) VICMA
Hair/Eyes/Mouth: Black rooted hair/brown sleep eyes/open-closed mouth with molded tongue
Clothing: Redressed
Value: $75
Photograph courtesy of Karen Kilburn

Zambardon Corp.™ - *The One and Only*®, 1988
Material: Cream-colored vinyl with stuffed brown cloth body
Height: 20in (50.8cm)
Marks: 1988/Martin
Hair/Eyes/Mouth: Dark brown, rooted hair styled in three sections with several twists in each/molded, painted eyes/closed mouth
Clothing: Kente-cloth print dress with white eyelet collar and hem, white socks with Kente-cloth print trim, black shoes
Other: Doll sculpted after a real little girl, Tamika Martin; says several different phrases when back is pressed
Value: $75
Photograph courtesy of Angela Garrett Terry

98

Zapf™ - *Sue*®, *Colette*® Series, 1997, Germany
Material: Vinyl head, arms, legs; stuffed brown cloth body
Height: 19in (48.26cm)
Marks: (Head) Zapf logo, Max Zapf (Body) Zapf Creation tag
Hair/Eyes/Mouth: Black curly wig, two ponytails tied in fabric that matches trim of blouse/brown sleep eyes
Clothing: All original
Value: $150

Unknown Manufacturers

Georgette-Type, ca. 1970's
Material: Vinyl head, arms, and legs; tan cloth body
Height: 22in (55.88cm)
Hair/Eyes/Mouth: Light brown, rooted hair with two long braids/green sleep eyes/closed smiling mouth, black freckles
Clothing: Pink cotton dress with white eyelet trim (possibly redressed), replaced white vinyl shoes
Other: Eegee™ made Caucasian redhead twins *Georgie*® and *Georgette*® in 1971. This doll is identical to those dolls including the girl doll's hairstyle, freckles, green eyes, and one arm bent at elbow. This doll, however, does not bear the Eegee™ mark.
Value: $75

Stuffed vinyl (larger doll) and Magic Skin (smaller doll) dolls, ca. 1950s
Height: 17in (43.18cm); 14in (35.56cm)
Hair/Eyes/Mouth: Rooted, black hair/brown sleep eyes/open-closed mouths
Clothes: Plaid dresses, possibly redressed
Value: $50 each

Topsy-type ca. 1960's
Material: Vinyl with jointed arms, non-jointed legs
Height: 5in (12.7cm)
Marks: (Back) Japan
Hair/Eyes/Mouth: Black, rooted hair in ponytail with two braids, bangs/painted eyes/closed mouth
Clothing: Painted-on white socks and red shoes
Value: $20

Trunk Doll, ca. 1990's
Material: Porcelain head, hands, lower legs and feet; stuffed-cloth body
Height: 12in (30.48cm)
Hair/Eyes/Mouth: Black wig/brown stationary eyes/closed mouth
Clothing: Original dress with extra outfit and trunk
Value: $35
Photograph courtesy of Unistine Harris

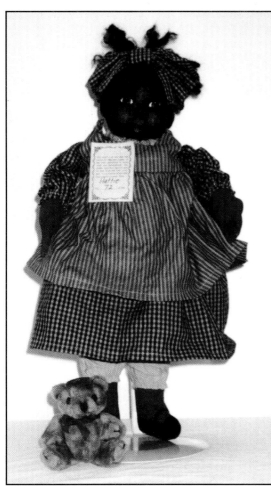

Maynard Arnett for The Country Store - *Hattie and Her Teddy* (1999), *Joy Christmas Doll* (2000), *Myrtis*, 1998
Material: Wood resin head; stuffed, cloth body with stitched hands to give appearance of fingers
Height: *Hattie* 19in (48.26cm); teddy bear 4in 10.16cm); *Joy* 20in (50.8cm); *Myrtis* 19½in (49.53cm)
Marks: (Body): CAM Hattie 72/500 *Arnett's Country Store* Head) #23 (Body) M *Joy* 23/150 (coat tag) *Joy* Head) M (body) M 149 © *Myrtis* 149/500
Hair/Eyes/Mouth: Dolls have mostly molded hair with wool-like material used for the applied hair/eyes, mouth, and nose are carved
Clothing: Clothing is all original and "aged"
Value: $150 each
Photograph Courtesy of Bonnie Lewis

Gwen Bentley, independent doll artist - *Nebi*, 2002
Material: Porcelain/stuffed-cloth body
Height: 29in (73.66cm)
Hair/Eyes/Mouth: Brown wig/brown eyes/closed mouth
Clothing: dressed by the owner
Other: Doll was made from a *Real People* mold
Value: $250
Photograph courtesy of Shirley Scott

Judy Boldon-Bain© for Caribbean Cultural Dolls,
Paradise Angel #4, 2001
Material: Wicker, natural colored raffia, and red cloth
Height: 12in (30.48cm)
Clothing: Red cloth headdress, woven natural-colored wicker dress with red and blue wicker at hem and red in sleeves; natural-colored raffia wings
Other: Doll came with accompanying note: "This handmade wicker and raffia Angel is the new addition to the Caribbean Cultural Dolls. It was inspired by and created to acknowledge the many heroes and victims of September 11, 2001. Designed and produced in the United States Virgin Islands."
Value: $85

Mary Carter, independent doll artist - *Danielle*, 1999
Material: Porcelain/stuffed-cloth body
Height: 30in (76.2cm)
Hair/Eyes/Mouth: Brown wig/brown eyes/closed mouth
Clothing: Dressed by the owner
Other: Doll made from a Donna RuBert mold
Value: $250
Photograph courtesy of Shirley Scott

Laura Cobabe - *Junior Dallas Cowboys Cheerleaders Collection, Dominique*, 1998
Material: Rigid vinyl
Height: 18½in (46.99cm)
Hair/Eyes/Mouth: Black wig/brown stationary eyes/applied eyelashes
Clothing: *Junior Dallas Cowboys Cheerleaders* outfit
Value: $100
Photograph courtesy of Deborah Daniels

Berdine Creedy for MasterPiece Gallery - *Leanna*, 2000
Material: Porcelain/stuffed cloth body
Height: 28in (71.12cm)
Marks: (Head) Berdine Creedy ©2000 #0229/1500 (hand numbered/signed in 18kt gold)
Hair/Eyes/Mouth: Brown wig/brown Pabol eyes, applied upper eyelashes
Clothing: Champagne-colored dress, ivory pantaloons, white socks, black patent-leather shoes
Other: Winner of *2000 Industries Choice DOTY Award*
Value: $175
Photograph courtesy of Manya R. Elliott

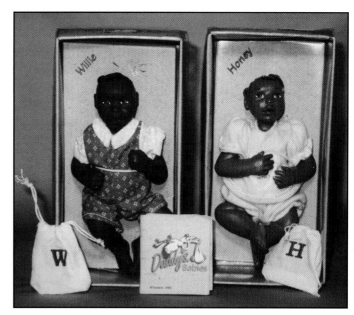

Karen Germany for Daddy's Babies® - *Willie* and *Honey*, 1999
Material: Resin
Height: 5in (12.7cm)
Marks: (Back) Daddy's® 1999
Hair/Eyes/Mouth: Molded resin hair/painted brown eyes
Clothing: Original clothing, drawstring bag with dolls' initials that contains toy
Value: $25 each

Karen Germany for Daddy's Long Legs - *Slats*, 1994
Material: Resin/cloth arms, legs
Height: 25in (63.5cm)
Hair/Eyes/Mouth: Painted brown eyes
Clothing: Baseball uniform with "DLL" patch; edition limit of 2323, retired in 1995
Value: $350
Photograph courtesy of Chelie Stambaugh

Karen Germany for Daddy's Long Legs - ***Wild Wood Will***, 1996
Material: Resin/cloth arms, legs
Height: 26in (66.04cm)
Hair/Eyes/Mouth: Black painted hair/brown painted eyes
Clothing: Complete cowboy outfit: genuine cowhide chaps, Western shirt, jeans, resin cowboy hat and boots, rope; LE 1000
Value: $575
Photograph courtesy of Chelie Stambaugh

Peggy Dey for Heavenly Treasures - *Jamaica*, 1997
Material: Vinyl/stuffed-cloth body
Height: 29in (73.66cm)
Marks: (Incised in neck) HTC 001/Peggy Dey/ (written/signed by artist) Jamaica #19/250 Peggy Dey (breastplate, signed and dated) Peggy Dey 10/25/97
Hair/Eyes/Mouth: Dark brown wig/brown stationary eyes, upper/lower eyelashes/open-closed mouth with two upper teeth
Clothing: Green and beige gingham, nautical-style dress, matching hat, white socks, black patent-leather shoes
Value: $450

Duck House - *Bella*, ca. 1990s
Material: Porcelain
Height: 21in (53.34cm)
Marks: LE 025/5000
Hair/Eyes/Mouth: Brown wig/brown, stationary eyes
Clothing: Original outfit
Value: $75
Photograph courtesy of Ruth Joyner

Bettina Feigenspan for Zapf Designer Collection - *Shawana*, 2000
Material: Vinyl/stuffed-cloth body
Height: 26in (66.04cm)
Marks: (Head) 16/B. Feigenspan Hirsh (Incised signature)
Hair/Eyes/Mouth: Multiple brown human hair braids with leather ties at ends/brown side-glancing, stationary eyes; upper and lower eyelashes
Clothing: Original outfit; holds an Annette Funicello Collectible Bear, *Butterscotch* (L. L. Knickerbocker, Inc.) and a ceramic vase; LE of 850 worldwide
Value: $600

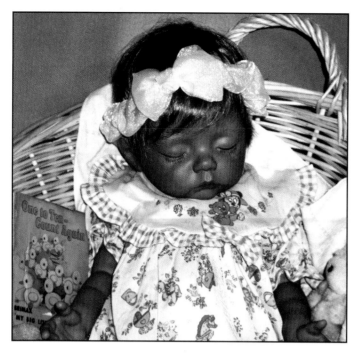

Mold by Dianna Effner, reproduction by Donna Flint - *Precious*, 1998
Material: Porcelain/stuffed-cloth body
Height: 22in (55.88cm)
Marks: (Incised in head) *Sleepy Head*/Dianna Effner/©1996 Expression
Hair/Eyes/Mouth: Auburn wispy wig/closed eyes; upper eyelashes
Clothing: Dressed by the artist, named by the author. This was the artist's first African-American porcelain doll
Value: $250

Marion Forek-Schmahl for Sigikid - *Katiba*, ca. 1994
Material: Vinyl/brown, stuffed-cloth body
Height: 23in (58.42cm)
Marks: (Head) 8/Sigikid/24581 MS 18/500
Hair/Eyes/Mouth: Black, curly wig accented with wooden discs, black and green painted eyes
Clothing: Original outfit; LE of 500
Other: *Katiba's* brother, *Wale*, was also made in 1994. According to *Katiba's* certificate, the fairy tale, the *Ten Little Negroes* was the artist's inspiration for the brother and sister pair.
Value: $550

Georgetown Collection - *Tyler, Boys will be Boys Collection*, 1997
Material: Porcelain/brown cloth body, upper arms/legs
Height: 14in (35.56cm)
Marks: Marked - Georgetown Collection/10th/Anniversary/Tyler ©MCMXCVII Georgetown Collection/(handwritten) TY4149
Hair/Eyes/Mouth: black wig/brown, side-glancing eyes
Clothing: White golf shirt with golf insignia, navy blue shoes, white socks, leather golf shoes; holds a golf club and tiny golf ball
Value: $100
Photograph courtesy of Karen Rae Mord

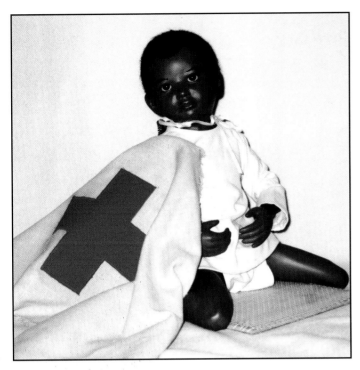

Jan Gipps, independent doll artist - *Ethiopian Boy*, 1989
Material: Porcelain/cloth body
Height: 13in (33.02cm) kneeling
Marks: Marked: Ethiopian Boy, artist's signature/
1989/2 (incised on back)
Hair/Eyes/Mouth: Applied curly hair on head and
eyebrows/brown glass eyes
Clothing: Original outfit and Red Cross blanket
Other: Inspired by photos of an Ethiopian refugee
child cared for by the Red Cross during the 1980s
famine crisis in Ethiopia. The original sale of doll went
to assist the Red Cross. Only two or three were made.
This doll is #2.
Value: $800
Photograph courtesy of Cheryl J. Bruce

Julie Good-Krüger for Good-Krüger Dolls -
Amity and *Puppy Love,* ca. 1992 and 1994
Material: Vinyl
Height: 20in (50.8cm) and 22in (55.88cm)
Marks: (Head, *Amity*) GK 930 Julie Good-
Krüger 1992 (hand signed and numbered by
the artist) (Head, *Puppy Love*) 4960 Julie
Good-Krüger
Hair/Eyes/Mouth: Black curly wigs/brown
stationary eyes
Clothing: Original outfits; *Amity* holds a bunny;
Puppy Love holds a basket of puppies. Both
have hangtags that bear the JGK logo and the
dolls' names.
Value: $225 each
Photograph courtesy of Debra Richardson

Julie Good-Krüger for Good-Krüger Dolls -
Snuggle Ebony, ca. 1994
Material: Vinyl/stuffed-cloth body
Height: 23in (58.42cm)
Marks: Hand signed: Julie Good Krüger #442
Hair/Eyes/Mouth: Black wig/brown eyes,
open/closed mouth
Clothing: Original pink velour romper, white
hat
Value: $300

Joke Grobben for Götz Puppenmanufaktur, *Michanou*, 2001
Material: Vinyl/stuffed and weighted velour body/upper arms
Height: 27in (68.58cm)
Marks: (Rear breastplate) Götz 255 (stomach, handwritten) #167/1000 2001
Hair/Eyes/Mouth: Dark brown, human hair wig/dark brown, handmade crystal eyes with single positioned eyelashes
Clothing: Two-piece orange silk outfit accented with blue, pink, green and orange threads; leather, laced sandals, beaded ponytail holder and Gotz bracelet
Value: $800
Photograph courtesy of Manya R. Elliott

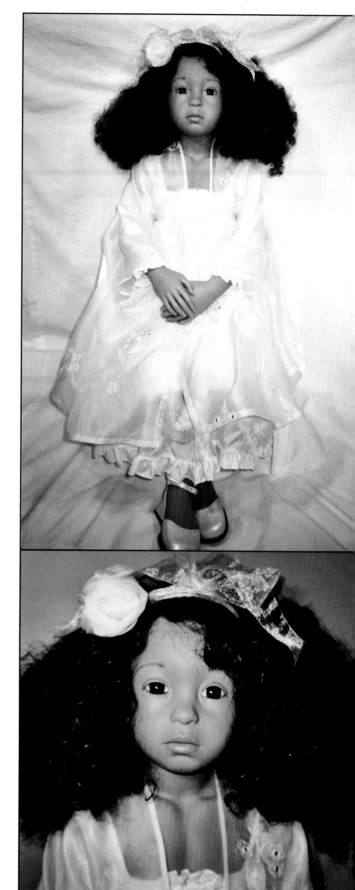

Philip Heath for Götz - *Angelica* "The Ultimate Collection" ca. 1999
Material: Vinyl head, torso, arms and lower legs; stuffed cloth buttocks and upper legs
Height: 38in (96.52cm)
Marks: (Head) PSH/444 24
Hair/Eyes/Mouth: Dark brown, natural-looking curly wig with fabric flower headband/brown eyes; applied upper and lower eyelashes
Clothing: White satin sundress and voile duster; shoes were added
Other: Doll is #375 of 750, has very lifelike detailed hands and feet. Has armature in arms and legs, highly poseable, can sit or stand.
Value: $1700

Philip Heath for Philip Heath Designs - *Petunia*, 1970
Material: Porcelain/stuffed-cloth body, upper arms and legs
Height: 8in (20.32cm)
Marks: (Head) Philip Heath 1970 England
Hair/Eyes/Mouth: Painted hair, brown eyes
Clothing: Dusty rose outfit with antique lace trim, matching bonnet, has the letter "P" on front of top, uncertain if clothing is original
Other: The owner named the doll
Value: $350
Photograph courtesy of Karen Rae Mord

Philip Heath for Götz - *Seraphina*, 1997 *Children of the World* series
Material: Vinyl/cloth body, above knees, and elbows
Height: 24in (60.96cm)
Hair/Eyes/Mouth: Long black wig/brown eyes
Clothing: White embroidered dress covered with a voile/chiffon overskirt; a white duster of the same fabric covers the dress, bare feet
Value: $1200
Photograph courtesy of Cheryl J. Bruce

Philip Heath for Philip Heath Designs - **Stephanie,**
Renaissance Collection, 2001, Limited Edition of 250
Material: Ebony artist vinyl (torso), lower arms/legs,
stuffed-cloth hips, sculptured buttocks/upper thighs
Height: 20in (50.8cm)
Marks: (Torso marked) PSH
Hair/Eyes/Mouth: Black wig/glass eyes
Clothing: Original outfit
Value: $500
Photograph Courtesy of Bonnie Lewis

Philip Heath for Philip Heath Designs - *Will*, 1997
Children of the World series
Height: 24in (60.96cm)
Hair/Eyes/Mouth: Molded hair/brown
stationary/closed, pursed lips
Clothing: All original outfit
Value: $1200
Photograph courtesy of Cheryl J. Bruce

Annette Himstedt for Timeless Creations - (Left to right) *Ayoka* (1986) 27in (68.58cm) represents a little girl from Africa. *Fatou* (1987) 26in (66.04cm) represents a 9-year-old child from Senegal. *Sanga* and *Pemba* (1992/1993), 22in (55.88cm), represent children from Tennessee.
Marks: Annette Himstedt incised in head and/or backs/limbs
Hair/Eyes/Mouth: Human hair/stationary eyes
Clothing: All original outfits
Values: $1000, $750, $350, $350 respectively

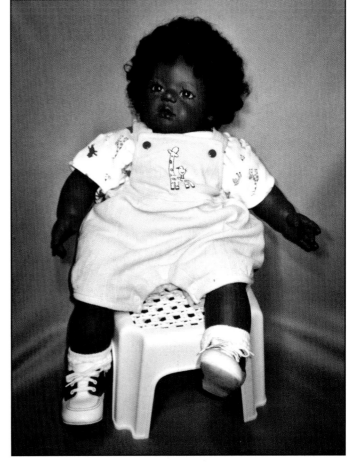

Annette Himstedt for Timeless Creations - *Baby Mo* (1989-1990) 22in (55.88cm) represents a 1-year-old, African-American baby
Marks: Annette Himstedt incised in head and/or backs/limbs
Hair/Eyes/Mouth: Human hair/stationary eyes
Value: $600

111

Annette Himstedt for Puppen Kinder® Collection - (Left to right) *Kerry* (1998) 23in (58.42cm) represents a 4-year-old girl, and *Baby Sunny Boy* (2001) 20in (50.8cm)
Marks: Annette Himstedt incised in head and/or backs/limbs
Hair/Eyes/Mouth: Human hair/stationary eyes
Value: $600 and $500 respectively

Annette Himstedt for Puppen Kinder® Collection - *Amber* (1999) represents a 7-year-old, Jamaican girl of the 1970s
Marks: Annette Himstedt incised in head and/or back/limbs
Hair/Eyes/Mouth: Human hair/stationary eyes
Value: $1200

Kathryn Hitchcock, independent doll artist -
DebZee, 1998
Material: Porcelain, weighted cloth body, upper
arms and legs (articulated)
Height: 15in seated (38.1cm)
Marks:
Hair/Eyes/Mouth: Black, curly wig/dark brown,
stationary eyes; applied upper eyelashes
Clothing: Lavender and white print dress, original
hand-smocked collar in shades of lavender on
white eyelet fabric, white infant socks with bows
Other: Doll, named by the collector, was received
from the artist in exchange for voice and piano
lessons
Value: $650
Photograph courtesy of Karen Rae Mord

Cliff Jackson for Ashton Drake Galleries - **Brianne** (1997), **Jacob** (1998), and **Tamara** (1998)
Material: Porcelain heads, arms and legs; cloth bodies
Height: 9in (22.86cm) seated
Marks: (Head) *Brianne* MTA0343, *Jacob* 3312FA and *Tamara* 1332FA
Hair/Eyes/Mouth: *Brianne* and *Jacob* - dark brown wigs, *Tamara* - black wig/brown stationary
eyes/smiling mouths with porcelain teeth
Clothing: all original clothing
Other: Mr. Jackson is an AA artist. These dolls are the first issue of his "Sunday's Best"
series.
Value: $125 each
Photograph courtesy of Debra Richardson

Jerri McCloud for Dolls by Jerri - *Portia*, ca. 1995
Material: Vinyl head, arms and legs; stuffed, brown cloth body
Height: 22in (55.88cm)
Marks: (Head marks) Jerri/91 V8C
Hair/Eyes/Mouth: Dark brown, curly wig styled in two ponytails/light brown, stationary eyes; applied upper eyelashes
Clothing: Peach voile dress with lace trim, white lace socks, white leatherette shoes
Value: $250

Ping Lau, independent doll artist - *Eboli and Babies* (OOAK dolls), 2001 and 2002
Material: Polymer clay
Height: (Left to right) 1in (2.54cm), 3½in (8.89cm), 8in (20.32cm) and 2in (5.08cm)
Hair/Eyes/Mouth: (Eboli) hand-knotted yarn hair, painted brown eyes; (babies) painted hair and eyes
Clothing: (*Eboli*) Afrocentric dress with beaded bracelets, anklets, and necklace; babies are nude. Tiniest baby is inside a walnut shell.
Other: *Eboli* and standing boy are from the "2001 D.C. Doll Expo." Sitting boy and baby in walnut are from the 2002 Expo
Value: $35, $50, $150 and $50 respectively
Photograph courtesy of Cheryl J. Bruce

B.K. Lee for Seymour Mann, *Engrid*, 1997
Material: Porcelain/stuffed-cloth body, upper arms and legs
Height: 18in (45.72cm)
Hair/Eyes/Mouth: Black mohair wig/brown stationary eyes; applied upper eyelashes
Clothing: All original cream-colored dress, white knee socks, brown, faux leather, lace-up boots; carries white bear
Other: Received double nomination for the *1997 Dolls of Excellence Award* and the *DOTY Award* (won the 1997 DOTY Award)
Value: $200
Photograph courtesy of Manya R. Elliott

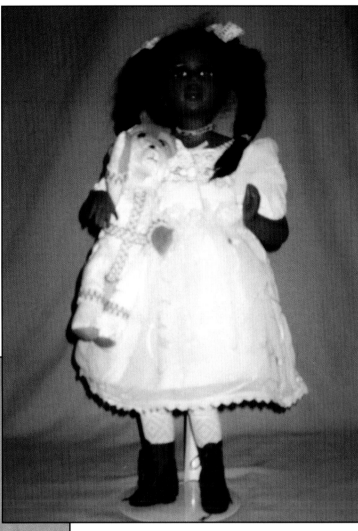

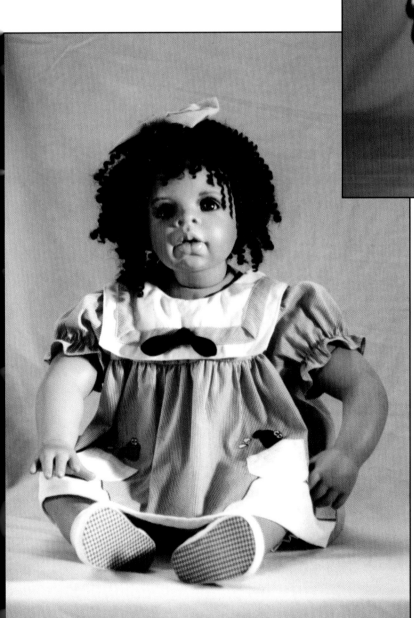

Monika Levening for MasterPiece Gallery - *Maria*, 2001
Material: Porcelain/brown fabric, weighted lower torso
Height: 16in seated (40.64cm)
Marks: (Head) Monika Levening (signature in gold) ©2001 #081/600
Hair/Eyes/Mouth: Black corkscrew curled wig/medium brown, stationary eyes with applied upper eyelashes
Clothing: All original red/white nautical-style dress
Value: $350
Photograph courtesy of Karen Rae Mord

Carin Lossnitzer for Götz - *Filipo* (a Carlos Dribble Baby), 1998
Material: Vinyl head, lower arms and legs; stuffed cloth body, pellet-stuffed upper arms and legs
Height: 23½in (59.69cm)
Marks: (Head) Carlos/Götz
Hair/Eyes/Mouth: Reddish-brown, curly, mohair wig/brown, blown glass eyes
Clothing: Wears original, multicolored Spanish-style outfit
Value: $450

Patricia Loveless for World Gallery of Dolls - *Camisha*, 1995
Material: Porcelain
Height: 19in (48.26cm)
Marks: (Head) Patricia Loveless 1995 0700/2000
Hair/Eyes/Mouth: Black wig with braids in front/brown stationary eyes
Clothing: Multicolored long jacket, pants, matching hat, black shoes
Value: $200
Photograph courtesy of Valerie Myers

Maria Rossi for Marigio Doll Creations - *Black Angioletto,* 2001
Material: Porcelain
Height: 4in (10.16cm)
Hair/Eyes/Mouth: Wool wig/painted brown eyes
Clothing: Ecru lace and voile dress, holds tiny flowered garland that matches headband, golden wings; LE #2 of 500
Value: $100
Photograph courtesy of Cheryl J. Bruce

Jan McLean for Jan McLean Originals - **Grace** standing and sitting, 2001
Material: Vinyl; stuffed cloth torso, upper arms and legs with armature for posing
Height: 21in (53.34cm) (Standing)
Marks: Jan McLean Designs (stamped signature)
Hair/Eyes/Mouth: Auburn mohair wig styled in a topknot with bangs; (sitting) styled in two loose ponytails with bangs; hazel, stationary eyes, applied upper eyelashes; closed mouth with natural lip color and liner
Clothing: Clothing is all original
Other: Both have French manicured nails. Standing doll was winner of Australian *Doll of the Year 2001* and *2001 Dolls of Excellence* awards.
Value: $250

Lee Middleton for Lee Middleton Original Dolls, Inc. -
Angel Kisses Boy and **Girl**, 1994
Material: All vinyl
Height: 14in (35.56cm) boy stands on tip toes; girl's feet are flat
Marks: (Head) Lee Middleton 1993, symbol of fish, hand-signed by Lee Middleton and numbered #57 (boy) #176 (girl)
Hair/Eyes/Mouth: Both have light brown wigs with gold tone, metal halos attached/brown stationary eyes/lips puckered in a kissing position
Clothing: White gowns with golden wings attached on back; girl's gown is long, boy's is short; bare feet; boy has slingshot
Value: $150 each

Lee Middleton for Lee Middleton Original Dolls, Inc. -
My Own Baby, 1994
Material: Vinyl head, hands and feet; stuffed-cloth body, upper arms and legs
Height: 20in (50.8cm)
Marks: (Incised in head) 081094 ©Lee Middleton 1994 (Fish Symbol) USA (hand signed and numbered) Lee Middleton 396/2000 (A warning against copying the doll is also incised in the doll's head)
Hair/Eyes/Mouth: Dark brown, wispy wig/closed eyes with applied upper eyelashes/open mouth to accommodate pacifier
Clothing: Pink infant's drawstring gown, white knit hat, disposable diaper; doll came with a mini Bible
Other: The author's daughter wore the fleece jacket and bunting in 1977
Value: $150

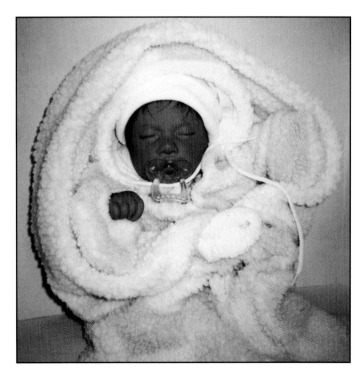

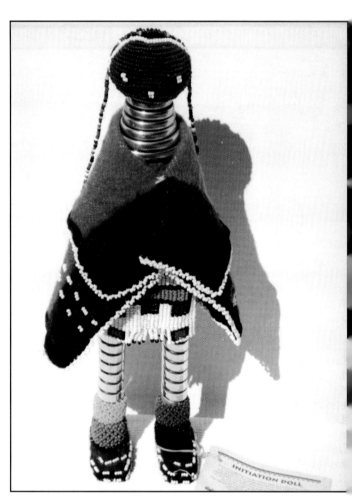

Reva Schick for Lee Middleton Original Dolls, Inc. - *Pamper's Kid*, 2001
Material: Vinyl head, arms, and full legs; cloth body
Height: 22in (55.88cm)
Marks: (Head) 1999 Lee Middleton Original Dolls by Reva Schick (signed and numbered by the artist) #253
Hair/Eyes/Mouth: Dark brown wig styled in two ponytails with bangs/dark brown stationary eyes with applied lashes
Clothing: All original clothing, came with bottle of fake spilled milk
Value: $200

Christine Orange for Elite Dolls, HSN - *Beth* and *Hiliary*, 2001
Material: Vinyl/cloth body
Height: 34in (86.36cm); 32in (81.28cm)
Marks: (Neck) Incision of artist's signature (Back) 2
Hair/Eyes/Mouth: (*Beth*) Brown, long curly wig replaces doll's original auburn wig; hazel stationary eyes. (*Hiliary*) Brown, curly wig; brown stationary eyes.
Clothing: (*Beth*) Green sateen dress and shoes. (*Hiliary*) Redressed in child's romper; wears original off-white sateen shoes. *Hiliary's* original dress is off-white sateen with stitched designs at bodice.
Value: $150 each

The Ndebele Tribeswomen - *Initiation Doll*, Africa, ca. 1996
Material: Constructed of metal, beads, cloth, faux leather. Face, hair, eyes, mouth constructed of multiple beads. Multiple silver neck rings, wool blanket wraps around torso, beaded apron skirt with faux leather back, multiple beads at ankles and on shoes
Height: 14½in (36.83cm)
Other: Hangtag reads: "This exquisitely handcrafted doll from Southern Africa is made by the tribeswomen of the Ndebele tribe. It is given to a girl after the initiation ceremony, which celebrates her reaching 'teenagehood.' It means that she is now old enough to be a mother. It is wished that she should marry a man as handsome as the doll. The glass, beaded apron symbolizes the happy marriage. The blanket is for warmth in the future."
Value: $150

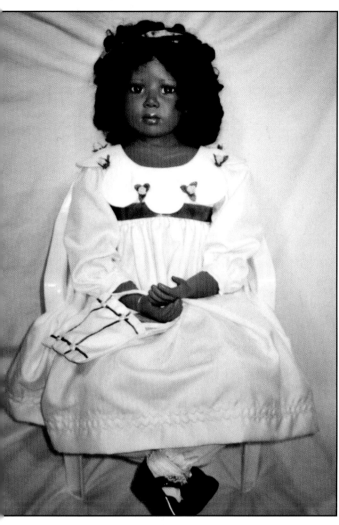

Anne Osman, independent doll artist -
Jahmelia, 2001
Material: Porcelain head, shoulder plate, arms
and legs; bean-filled Kapok armatured body
Height: 27in (68.58cm)
Hair/Eyes/Mouth: Brunette human-hair braided
wig with beads/brown stationary glass eyes
Clothing: Afrocentric outfit
Other: Made exclusively for the Camberley
Doll and Bear Shop - England; came with LE
Robin Rive (New Zealand) Golly
Value: $800
Photograph courtesy of Cheryl J. Bruce

Christine Orange for Elite Dolls, HSN - *Maya*, 2001
Material: Porcelain head, arms, legs; stuffed-cloth body
Height: 36in (91.44cm)
Marks: Hand signed and numbered: Christine Orange
412/2000
Hair/Eyes/Mouth: Brunette, curly wig/brown stationary
eyes/breather nose
Clothing: White dress with sage green piping at
bodice; cloth white flowers accent collar, white
pantaloons, matching handbag; purple patent-leather
shoes
Value: $200

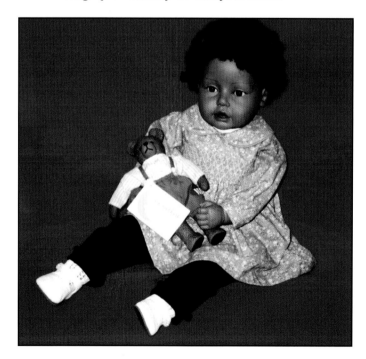

Heidi Ott for Heidi Ott® - *Baby Georgia*, 2000
Material: Vinyl head, arms and legs; stuffed, pellet-
weighted cloth body
Height: 29in (73.66cm)
Marks: (Head) Heidi Ott 2000 96/250 (written) Heidi
Ott (incised)
Hair/Eyes/Mouth: Brown, human hair afro wig with tiny
braids accented with fuchsia beads/brown stationary
eyes
Clothing: Original outfit
Other: Brown, vinyl, jointed teddy bear came with doll
Value: $500

Martha Pineiro for Pineiro Dolls - **Tomiko**, 2000
Material: Vinyl
Height: 30in (76.2cm)
Hair/Eyes/Mouth: Red mohair wig/green eyes/open mouth with teeth
Clothing: Cream-colored top with peach skirt; feather necklace, carries shoulder bag
Other: Characteristic Pineiro star molded on right hand
Value: $350
Photograph courtesy of Cheryl J. Bruce

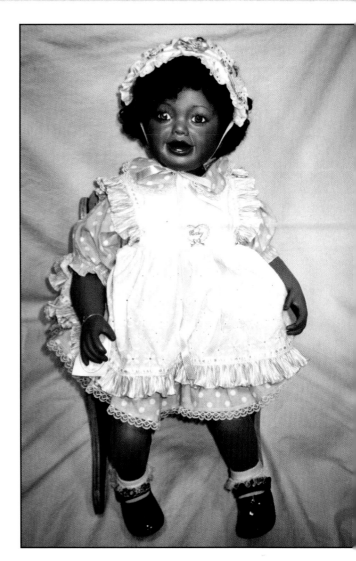

Rosemary Rhodes/Treasured Heirloom Collection - **Adora Rose**, ca. 1999
Material: Porcelain head, arms and legs; stuffed-cloth body
Height: 24in (60.96cm) seated
Marks: Hand signed, Rosemary Rhodes 0126/2000
Hair/Eyes/Mouth: Black, curly wig/green stationary eyes, applied upper/lower eyelashes/open, smiling mouth with two lower teeth
Clothing: All original outfit
Value: $150

Rosemary Rhodes for Elite Dolls - **Veronika**, 2002
Material: Vinyl head, lower arms and lower legs; stuffed, weighted-cloth body, upper arms and upper legs
Height: 31in (78.74cm)
Marks: (Head, signature) Rosemary Rhodes 314/1000
Hair/Eyes/Mouth: Dark brown wispy wig/brown stationary eyes; applied upper eyelashes
Clothing: Pink romper and shirt, pink snowsuit
Value: $75

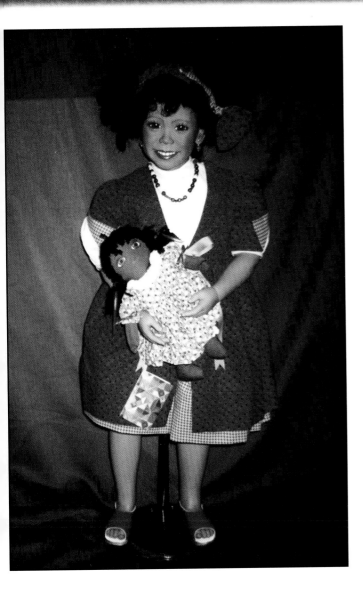

Bruno Rossellini for Great American Doll Company (GADCO) - *Madison Mandela* with Black cloth doll, 1997
Material: Vinyl with stuffed cloth body and upper legs, has armature
Height: 32in (81.28cm)
Marks: (Incised in head) The Great American Doll Company an Original Bruno Rossellini Design (Handwritten) 801/1500
Hair/Eyes/Mouth: Wears black, curly wig styled in two ponytails/brown stationary eyes; applied upper/lower eyelashes/smiling mouth with six individually painted teeth
Clothing: All original outfit
Value: $400

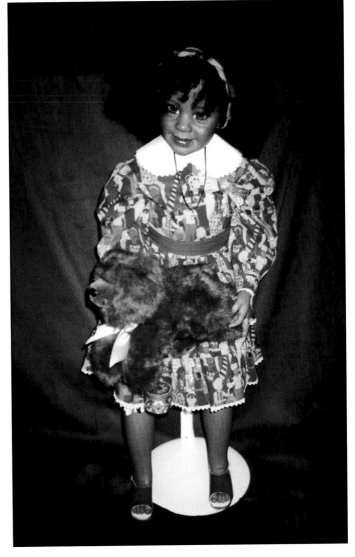

Bruno Rossellini for Great American Doll Company (GADCO) - *Shoshana II* (Chairman's Special Edition), ca. late 1990s
Material: Vinyl with stuffed cloth body and upper legs, has armature for posing
Height: 33in (83.82cm)
Marks: (Incised in head) The Great American Doll Company an Original Bruno Rossellini Design (Handwritten) 18/50
Hair/Eyes/Mouth: Wears loose, floppy afro wig/brown stationary eyes with applied upper and lower eyelashes/smiling closed mouth
Clothing: Kwanzaa celebration dress; gold teddy bear pendant with one-point diamond; blue leather shoes, holds Kwanzaa gift box, and 12-inch, mink-like fur teddy
Value: $400

Kelly Rubert for Doll Artworks - *Jamaica*, 1998
Material: Porcelain with stuffed-cloth body
Height: 25in (63.5cm)
Marks: (Head) Stamped gold signature: Kelly J. RuBert ©1998. Written: 0373/2000.
Hair/Eyes/Mouth: Black long curly wig, blue-gray stationary eyes
Clothing: All original outfit
Value: $250

Val Shelton for Val Shelton Originals - *Shaila*, ca. 1995
Material: Vinyl/stuffed cloth body
Height: 24in (60.96cm)
Marks: (Head) ©1994 Val Shelton
Hair/Eyes/Mouth: Dark brown cornrows with white beads/brown stationary eyes; applied upper/lower eyelashes
Clothing: Yellow floral romper, white lace socks, black patent-leather shoes
Value: $200

FayZah Spanos for Artist Collectibles-*Buttercup*, ca. 1992
Material: All vinyl
Height: 20in (50.8cm)
Marks: (Head) *Baby Ballerina* Fayzah Spanos ©1991 Artist Collectibles
Hair/Eyes/Mouth: Black wig styled in two ponytails with bangs/brown stationary eyes; applied upper and painted lower eyelashes/open-closed smiling mouth with molded tongue and two upper and two lower teeth
Clothing: Yellow, lace-trimmed frilly dress; matching pantaloons, white socks, white shoes
Other: This doll was made before the artist formed her own company
Value: $250

Fayzah Spanos for Precious Heirloom-*Corine* a.k.a. *Corina*, ca. 1996
Material: Vinyl/cloth body and upper legs
Height: 27in (68.58cm)
Marks: (Head) A Fayzah Spanos Design 1994
Hair/Eyes/Mouth: Brunette hair styled in two long braids with curls at sides of face/green stationary eyes; applied upper/lower eyelashes
Clothing: White eyelet, full-length dress; white pantaloons, bare feet; jointed bear came with doll
Value: $250

Fayzah Spanos for Precious Heirloom - **Kenyata**, ca. 1996 and **Wild About You**, 2001
Material: (*Kenyata*) Vinyl head, arms almost to shoulder, legs below knee; cloth body and upper legs; (*Wild About You*) All vinyl
Height: Both dolls are 26in (66.04cm)
Marks: (*Kenyata*) Fayzah Spanos 1996; (*Wild About You* head) Fayzah Spanos 171/500
Hair/Eyes/Mouth: (*Kenyata*) Braided hair/brown stationary eyes; applied eyelashes. (*Wild About You*) Brunette hair/hazel stationary eyes
Clothing: (*Kenyata*) Ethnic print outfit with matching headdress; (*Wild About You*) Ethnic style outfit, head wrap, cape with removable wings
Value: $300 each
Photograph courtesy of Debra Richardson

Fayzah Spanos for Precious Heirloom - **Prim and Proper**, 2000
Material: Vinyl head, arms and legs; stuffed cloth body
Height: 30in (76.2cm)
Marks: (Head) Fayzah Spanos Design 1995, signed and numbered behind left ear "Fayzah Spanos 2000"
Hair/Eyes/Mouth: Dark brown upswept wig/slightly side-glancing, hazel, stationary eyes; applied upper/lower eyelashes
Clothing: Mint green dress, ivory crocheted handbag with rose accent, off-white, patent-leather shoes. LE of 300, sold through HSN
Value: $350

Ruth Treffeisen for Ruth Treffeisen® - *Aimee*, ca. 1996
Material: Vinyl/stuffed-cloth body
Height: 30in (76.2cm)
Marks: (Head) Ruth Treffeisen ©1996
Hair/Eyes/Mouth: Black wig/brown stationary eyes, applied upper and lower eyelashes/closed mouth
Clothing: Original outfit except Aimee's original navy blue socks have been replaced with ivory-colored lace-trimmed socks
Value: $750

William Tung for Tuss, Inc. - *Mary, The Church Lady*, 1998
Material: Porcelain/brown stuffed-cloth body
Height: 20in (50.8cm)
Marks: (Back, signed) W. Tung 1998
Hair/Eyes/Mouth: Black, long wig/brown, glass eyes; applied upper and lower eyelashes/closed mouth
Clothing: Black two-piece suit custom designed by Anthony Mark Hankins (AA fashion designer), holds handbag and the leash of dog, Barkley. Has large hatbox with Anthony Mark Hankins' signature, Paris, Dallas and New York on front
Value: $100
Photograph courtesy of Freda Goldston

127

Virginia Erhlich Turner for Artists Collectibles - *Molly*, 1993
Material: All vinyl
Height: 20in (50.8cm)
Marks: (Head) Virginia E. Turner (signature) 247/2500 (written) ©1989 V. Ehrlich Turner (signature incised)
Hair/Eyes/Mouth: Black wig/brown stationary eyes with applied upper eyelashes, painted lower eyelashes/open-closed, smiling mouth with molded tongue; two painted upper and two lower teeth
Clothing: Original romper, socks, and shoes; faux diamond earrings
Value: $250

Mary Van Osdell for Premiere Artists Collection - *Josephine* (mold fired by Angie's Doll Boutique, Inc.), 2002
Material: Porcelain/cloth body
Height: 19in (48.26cm)
Marks: (Head) Angie's Doll Boutique, Inc., Alexandria, VA 06/2002
Hair/Eyes/Mouth: Black curly wig/closed eyes/smiling mouth
Clothing: Wears infant's dress, socks and shoes
Other: Doll kit and cloth body put together/sewn by Debra Richardson
Value: $100

Mary Van Osdell for Premiere Artists Collection - *Mercedes*, ca. 1995
Material: Porcelain/cloth body
Height: 21in (53.34cm) seated outside of car; 24in (60.96cm) seated inside car
Marks: (Back) Mary Van Osdell 0292/1000 (hand numbered)
Hair/Eyes/Mouth: Synthetic dark brown wig/dark brown eyes with applied upper lashes/closed mouth
Clothing: Original 1930s-style outfit; has rag doll
Value: $325
Photograph courtesy of Manya R. Elliott

Mary Van Osdell for Premiere Artist Collection - *Sissy*
and *Elmo* doll made from MVO kit
Material: Porcelain/cloth bodies
Height: *Sissy* 24in (60.96cm); *Elmo* 23in (58.42cm)
Marks: *Sissy*: (Head) Incised and stamped signature,
written edition number: Mary Van Osdell/ 0268/2000.
Elmo: (Head) Lynn M. Reid/Angie's 07/01/02; (Back
breastplate, faintly visible) A Mary Van Osdell Original
Doll
Hair/Eyes/Mouth: *(Sissy)* Black wig styled in two plaits
with curly bangs/brown, stationary eyes; applied upper
eyelashes/smiling mouth, showing off her new front
tooth *(Elmo)* Short curly afro wig, sized to fit/ brown,
stationary eyes/mouth is closed
Clothing: *(Sissy)* Original outfit. *(Elmo)* Outfit made from
Elmo pattern. Holds flower.
Other: *Elmo*'s kit was put together by Debra Richardson
Value: $200 each

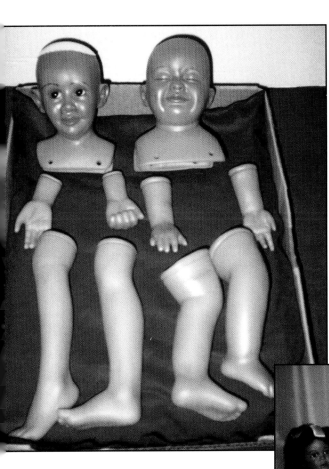

Mary Van Osdell's *Elmo* and *Josephine* doll kits
purchased from Angie's Doll Boutique, Inc.,
Alexandria, VA, before the kits were put together
by Debra Richardson
Photograph courtesy of Debra Richardson

Mary Van Osdell Dolls on Display (Left to
right) *Cupcake* 23in (58.42cm), *Petunia*
24in (60.96cm), *Maybelline* 28in
(71.12cm), *Lucinda* 17in (43.18 cm)
holding *Sweet Pea* 10½in (26.67 cm),
Lucinda 23in (58.42cm), and *Dot* 24in
(60.96 cm).
Photograph courtesy of Debra Richardson

Mary Van Osdell for Premiere Artist Collection - *Walter*, ca. 1995
Material: Porcelain/cloth body
Height: 24in (60.96cm)
Marks: (Head) Incised and stamped signature, written edition number: Mary Van Osdell/ 0788/2000
Hair/Eyes/ Mouth: Black wig/brown stationary eyes, applied upper eyelashes/ closed mouth
Clothing: All original outfit, socks, shoes, holds yo-yo
Value: $200

"*Great Lives Observed*"

Historic Tradition of Black Women

130

Opposite page: Mary E. Washington, independent doll artist - **Great Lives Observed (GLO)** and **Historic Tradition of Black Women (HTBW)** series, ca. 1990
Material: Porcelain heads and limbs, cloth bodies
Height: All *GLO* are 21in (53.34cm) except Thurgood Marshall - 22in (55.88cm); *HTBW:* 19in - 21in (48.26 -53.34cm)
Marks: (Bodies) signed and dated. *GLO*
Clothing: Dressed by the artist in first-quality fabrics and accessories with quality craftsmanship. *GLO* dolls. (Left to right) Thurgood Marshall, Dr. Mary McLeod Bethune, Frederick Douglass, and Madam C. J. Walker. *HTBW* dolls. (Left to right) Sojourner Truth, Harriet Tubman, Mahalia Jackson, the Storyteller. Ms. Washington's original creations come with a brief history of each doll.
Value: (*GLO*) $500 each, (*HTBW*) $300-350
Photograph courtesy of Mary E. Washington, artist

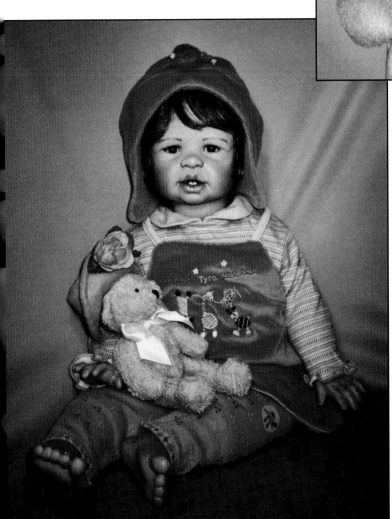

Kaye Wiggs for MasterPiece Gallery - **Tabitha**, 2001
Material: Porcelain/cloth body
Height: 21in (53.34cm)
Marks: (Head) Kaye Wiggs ©2001 #0466 of 1500
Hair/Eyes/Mouth: Brown wig and eyes
Clothing: Original outfit, holds terry cloth puppy
Other: *2001 Doll of the Year* nominee; second doll in the *Circle of Love Continuity* series
Value: $250
Photograph courtesy of Chelie Stambaugh

Kaye Wiggs for MasterPiece Gallery - **Tyra**, 2002
Material: Porcelain/cloth body
Height: 22in (55.88cm)
Marks: (Head) Kaye Wiggs (incised), gold signature; 053/500
Hair/Eyes/Mouth: Light brown wispy wig/brown stationary eyes/open-closed mouth with two upper teeth
Clothing: Original clothing, beige teddy bear
Value: $150

Goldie Wilson for HSN - *Adashia*, 2002
Material: Porcelain/cloth body
Height: 30in (76.2cm)
Marks: (Head) Goldie Wilson (signature) ©2002 052/200, LE doll
Hair/Eyes/Mouth: Black hair/brown eyes; heavily applied upper and lower eyelashes/breather/closed mouth
Clothing: Original ethnic print dress, hat, brown sandals
Value: $150

Alice Wolleydt for World Gallery of Dolls - *Katrina, Children in Portraiture Series,* 1993
Material: Porcelain/cloth body
Height: 25in (63.5cm)
Marks: (Head marks) *Katelynn*/©1993 Holly J.
Hair/Eyes/Mouth: Brunette wig/green eyes, upper and lower eyelashes/open-closed mouth
Clothing: Original outfit
Value: $200

Unmarked doll affectionately called *Pop*, ca. 1996
Material: Porcelain
Height: 18in (45.72cm)
Hair/Eyes/Mouth: Molded hair/brown eyes
Clothing: Redressed
Other: This doll bears a marked resemblance to the collector's father. The doll sparked her interest in collecting.
Value: $100
Photograph courtesy of Shirley Scott

CHAPTER 6

Personality/Celebrity Dolls

Daddy's (KVK, Inc.) - **Anthony Mark Hankins "Soul Anthony"** (2002) a Home Shopping Network exclusive
Material: Resin head/torso, arms, and legs/cloth body, poseable
Height: 25in (63.5cm)
Hair/Eyes/Mouth: Painted black, realistic-looking dreadlocks; black beard/brown eyes
Clothing: Wears a white, two-piece pants set, accented with a gold braided sash; multiple golden chains, cross, and bracelet; bare feet
Other: Comes with hangtag and a window display, monogrammed box
Value: $60

Effanbee - **Muhammad Ali** (1986) from the "I am the Greatest" *Great Moments in Sports*, Series #7652, made for one year only
Material: All vinyl, jointed doll
Height: 18in (45.72cm) in boxer's stance
Marks: (Head marks) Effanbee 1986 M. Ali.
Hair/Eyes/Mouth: Molded black hair/painted eyes
Clothing: Wears replica of Everlast white satin, red-trimmed boxing trunks with matching robe, boxing gloves, white faux leather boxing shoes
Other: Instructions for posing and a signed letter from Muhammad Ali accompany the doll
Value: $250

133

Galoob Direct, Inc. - *Mel B Spice Girls #1* (1997), *Spice Girls on Tour* (1998), *Spice Girls Concert Collection* (1998)
Material: All vinyl
Height: 11½in (29.21cm)
Hair/Eyes/Mouth: Brown rooted natural textured hair with golden highlights/painted brown eyes/ open-closed mouth with painted teeth
Clothing: Outfits: Leopard top and pants, zebra jacket and shorts, orange top and shorts with sheer overtop and pantyhose
Value: $35 each

Hasbro - *Destiny's Child Kelly, Beyonce,* and *Michelle,* 2001
Material: All vinyl
Height: 11½in (29.21cm)
Hair/Eyes/Mouth: Rooted hair
Other: Represent the popular singing group
Value: $30 each
Photograph courtesy of Debra Richardson

Ideal Toy Corp - *Diana Ross* (1970)
Material: All vinyl
Height: 18in (45.72cm),
Marks: (Head) 1968 Ideal Toy Corp DR-18-H148. (Buttocks) 1969 Ideal Toy Corp GH-18 US Pat. #3,162, 976
Hair/Eyes/Mouth: Black rooted bubble cut hairstyle/open smiling mouth/painted teeth
Clothing: Original gold lamé gown with orange marabou feathers, gold vinyl *Crissy* shoes
Value: $100 (loose), $250 NRFB

Jazwares, Inc. (2002) - **Tina Thomas** *WNBA Houston Comets,* plastic water bottle
Height: 10in (25.4cm)
Hair/Eyes/Mouth: Molded braid with pink ponytail holder
Other: This is the first 3D water bottle created by the WNBA, LE 5000, given out at the July 25, 2002 *Comets* vs. *Miami Sol* game, won by the Comets 69-60. *Tina* holds a Sears breast cancer awareness pink and white ball. Top of water bottle contains a straw; top is removable.
Value: $50

Mattel™-*Brandy* (1999), a Kitty Black-Perkins doll for Mattel™
Material: All vinyl, jointed
Height: 11½in (29.21cm),
Hair/Eyes/Mouth: Multiple tiny braids and painted "baby" hair outlines face
Clothing: Wears orange skirt and top with extra shimmering orange pants; microphone, gold platform shoes, stand included
Value: $35

(L-R)-Mattel™ - **Stacey Dash as Dionne** (1996) in the TV series and movie, *Clueless* and Sindy/Hasbro™ - *Naomi Campbell* (1995) made for the European market
Material: Vinyl
Height: Both are 11½in (29.21cm)
Hair/Eyes/Mouth: (Stacey Dash as Dionne) Brown rooted braids/brown eyes; (Naomi Campbell) Long brunette rooted hair/brown painted eyes/open-closed mouth
Clothing: (Stacey Dash as Dionne) Wears lavender outfit, hat. Comes with cell phone, animal backpack, child's ring; (Naomi Campbell) Wears pink and black gown, matching earrings, bracelet. Stand, model profile and photo included.
Value: $30 and $50 respectively

Mattel™ - *Talking Julia* (1969)
Material: Vinyl
Height: 11½in (29.21cm)
Hair/Eyes/Mouth: Doll's rooted hair was originally brown, but turned red due to oxidation/brown painted eyes
Clothing: Doll wears original outfit and holds custom-made mink coat, fashioned from mink coat owned by doll owner's mother
Other: Based on the TV character *Julia*, starring actress Diahann Carroll, the first AA woman featured in her own TV series. Julia was made from the vintage *Christie*® a.k.a. *Midge*® mold.
Value: $80
Photograph courtesy of Lee Johnson

Mattel™, Saalfield™, and Colorforms™ - *Julia (Diahann Carroll)* dolls and paper dolls, based on the NBC TV series
Material: All vinyl
Height: 11½in (29.21cm)
Other: From (L-R) Boxed *Julia* paper dolls by Saalfield™, contains four dolls (*Julia, Corey, Marie* and *Earl J. Waggedorn*) and their outfits (49 costume pieces), MCMLXX (box), MCMLXVIII (costumes); *Talking Julia* doll by Mattel™ (1969), stock #1128 ; *Julia* dress-up kit by Colorforms™ (1969); *Julia* doll by Mattel™ (1969) in one-piece nurse outfit; and another boxed *Julia* paper doll set by Saalfield™ with same four dolls, same wardrobe, different box cover that reads "Authorized Edition.".
Values: Boxed paper dolls $50, talking doll $200, Colorforms™ doll $45, loose nurse doll $100

Nike, Inc.™ - *Little Penny* (1997), from the 1990s Nike TV Commercials with Penny Hardaway and *Little Penny* (the character)
Height: 14in (35.56cm)
Other: Has a push button in his back that activates talking mechanism, voice of comedian/actor Chris Rock. Came with a basketball scaled for the figure.
Value: $40

No Limit Toys - *Talking Master P* (ca. 1999)
Material: Vinyl head and hands, cloth body, legs, arms
Height: 17in (43.18cm)
Hair/Eyes/Mouth: Molded hair/painted brown eyes (wears sunglasses)/open-closed mouth with molded teeth
Clothing: Wears camouflage outfit, hat, gold chain necklace, molded brown shoes
Other: Squeeze to activate voice, says "Uh, na-na-na-na." Requires two AAA batteries.
Value: $40

Play Along - *Venus* and *Serena Williams* American *Champions* (2000).
Material: Vinyl
Height: Both dolls are 11½in (29.21cm)
Marks: (Back) ©1999 PA China
Hair/Eyes/Mouth: Painted eyes/smiling open mouths that show teeth
Clothing: All original tennis outfits with tennis accessories and COA
Value: $30 each

Triumph Entertainment - *Michael Jackson Street Life* (1997), sold in Europe
Clothing: Dressed in white shirt, black trousers, one white glove
Other: Push-button on back, comes with cassette. Push-button activates Jackson's "Black or White" song. A non-singing version was also made.
Value: $50
Photograph Courtesy of Michelle Hoskins

137

Paper Dolls

What fun we had as children playing with paper dolls, pretending that we were the dolls on whom the carefully cut or punched-out outfits were being placed. I remember slipping a paper doll book into the shopping cart on most grocery store trips with my parents. Upon reaching the checkout counter, these paper doll books prompted repeated surprise for my unsuspecting parents. Because they never made me put them back, this was a childhood routine conducted whenever I found a paper doll book that interested me.

Most of the paper dolls included in this chapter were photographed in groups. Each photograph is described from left to right and top to bottom, when necessary. The value of each paper doll is included following the descriptions for each. Unless otherwise stated, the paper dolls in this chapter are from my personal adult collection. Although the method by which they were acquired differs from my childhood acquisitions, they remind me of the fun I experienced acquiring my childhood paper dolls and of the fun I experienced pretending with them.

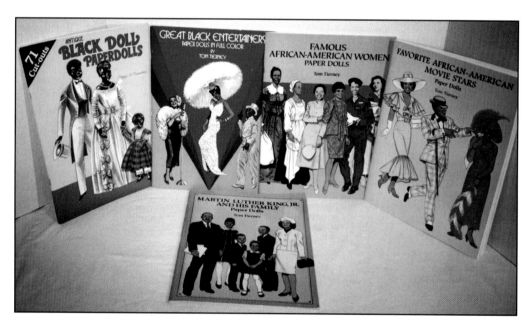

Antique Black Doll Paper Dolls by Peggy Jo Rosamond, Hobby House Press, 1991. Dolls and doll illustrations vary in size from 2in to 10in (5.08cm - 2.54cm). Period-appropriate outfits and dolls representing a circa 1930s composition baby, black Belton-type French bisque child, black china doll, black doll of papier-mâché, wooden lady doll, and black bisque baby doll. The 2-in dolls include two Norah Wellings™ dolls, Topsy-Turvey, Bruckner, two Leo Moss™ dolls, Steiff™, two primitives, Bru Lady and an SFBJ; they do not have outfits.

Great Black Entertainers Paper Dolls by Tom Tierney, Dover Publications, Inc., 1994. Paper dolls vary in size from 6in to 7in (15.24cm - 17.78cm). Includes paper dolls and outfits for Louis Armstrong, Josephine Baker, Dorothy Dandridge, Billie Holiday, Hattie McDaniel, Paul Robeson, Bill "Bo Jangles" Robinson, Bessie Smith, Ethel Waters, and Bert Williams.

Famous African-American Women Paper Dolls by Tom Tierney, Dover Publications, Inc., 1994. Dolls vary in size from 8in to 9in (20.32cm - 22.86cm). Includes paper dolls and outfits for Phyllis Wheatley, Sojourner Truth, Pauline Cushman, Madam C. J. Walker, Mary McLeod Bethune, Zora Neale Hurston, Rosa Parks, Patricia Roberts Harris, Shirley St. Hill Chisholm, Althea Gibson, Maya Angelou, Toni Morrison, Barbara Jordan, Judith Jamison, and Mae C. Jemison, M.D.

Favorite African-American Movie Stars by Tom Tierney, Dover Publications, Inc., 1997. Dolls vary in size from 8½in to 9½in (21.59cm - 24.13cm). Includes paper dolls and outfits worn by the stars in some of their roles: Angela Bassett, Ruby Dee, Laurence Fishburn, Morgan Freeman, Danny Glover, Whoopi Goldberg, Gregory Hines, Whitney Houston, Samuel L. Jackson, James Earl Jones, Diana Ross, Wesley Snipes, Cicely Tyson, Denzel Washington, Vanessa Lynn Williams, and Oprah Winfrey.

Martin Luther King, Jr., and His Family by Tom Tierney, Dover Publications, Inc., 1993. Dolls vary in size from 5½in to 9in (13.97cm - 22.86cm). Includes paper dolls and outfits for Dr. Martin Luther King, Jr.; his wife, Coretta Scott King; and their children: Yolanda, Martin Luther King, III., Dexter and Bernice King.
Value: $25 each

Barbie, Christie, Stacey, Whitman/Mattel™, 1968, includes three 10in (25.4cm) punch-out dolls with stands and punch-out clothing. *Groovy World of Barbie and Her Friends Paper Dolls*, Whitman/Mattel™ 1971, includes four 11½in (29.21cm) punch-out dolls with stands and clothing. *Barbie and Her Friends (Curtis and Cara) All Sports Tournament*. Whitman/Mattel™, 1975, *Cara®* and *Barbie®* are 9½in (24.13cm); *Curtis®* and *Ken®* are 10in (25.4cm). Each doll has several punch-out outfits and accessories.
Value: $25 each

Black Baby Articulated Paper Doll, Littauer and Bauer (Germany), ca. 1885, 9in (22.86cm) die cut doll with limbs secured by brass brads. Dolls were printed smiling or unsmiling and originally sold in envelopes with crepe and tissue paper in assorted colors for costuming.
Value: $150
Photograph courtesy of Arabella Grayson

Betty and Billy. 1955, Whitman Publishing Company, 9½in (24.13cm) doll. Several outfits for each doll, includes their dog Chum, his doghouse; and a Black doll for Betty. Original cost 10 cents.
Value: $50

Cuddly Baby, Whitman Publishing Division, 1969, includes 12in (30.48cm) baby doll with punch-out outfits. **Baby Doll**, Lowe, James and Jonathan, 1969, includes 10in (25.4cm) baby with simulated hair and outfits. **Baby Sue**, Lowe, James and Jonathan, 1969, includes 10in (25.4cm) baby (same baby as in *Baby Doll* by Lowe) with punch-out clothing. **Betty Doll**, Lowe, James and Jonathan, 1969, includes 11in (27.94cm) punch-out doll and clothing. ***Stand-Up Doll with Sew-on, Hole-punched dresses***, Samuel Lowe Company, ca. 1972, same doll as *Betty Doll*. 11in (27.94cm) precut doll with push-out dresses and yarn for lacing clothing to doll.
Value: $15 each

Dennis Rodman Bad as I Wanna Be the Unauthorized Dennis Rodman Paper Doll Book Parody, Cader Books, Three Rivers Press, 1997, 9in (22.86cm) paper doll with male and female outfits including a wedding gown and tuxedo.
Amazing Grace Paper Doll, Dial Books for Young Readers, 1998, 8in (20.32cm) paper doll with stand, several outfits.
Value: $15 each

Deb and Marcus Caleb Magnetic Paper Dolls, Wave Media Inc., 2000. These are customized 5½in (13.97cm) paper dolls made for the author and her grandson. Each paper doll comes with several outfits and a bedroom backdrop.
Value: $25 each

Double Date, Checkerboard Press, 1989, 8in (20.32cm) and 7½in (19.05cm) couples, one white and one black, precut dolls, clothes and accessories. *Friends at School*, Checkerboard Press, 1989, 9in (22.86cm) multicultural friends - an African American boy, a Caucasian girl and boy, and an Asian girl.
Value: $10 each

Effanbee's Patsyette Paper Dolls by John Axe, Hobby House Press 1997. Includes 9in (22.86cm) Black Patsy paper doll, stand, and outfits. Effanbee's Patsy Paper Doll Family by Peggy Jo Rosamond, Hobby House Press, 1997. Includes Black Patsyette and Black Patsyette Brother 6in (15.24cm) paper dolls, stand, and outfits.
Value: $10 each

The Happy Family Paper Dolls, Mattel/Whitman 1977, five dolls: father, mother, baby, grandfather, and grandmother. Father and grandfather are 9½in (24.13cm), mother and grandmother are 9in (22.86cm). Baby is 3in (7.62cm). Lydia Paper Doll, Whitman, 1976, 9½in (24.13cm) doll. Shirley Doll Cutout Book, Lowe, ca. 1970s, 6½in (16.51cm) doll. Yolanda, a Deana Doll by Deana Collins, 1985; a 2¼in (5.72cm) lithographed paper doll card. Each paper doll has several outfits and stands.
Value: $20, $15, $10, and $2 respectively

My Little Mahji Paper Doll Set, Velb Associates, 1981, 11½in (29.21cm) doll, designed by Laverne Hall. Paper doll was created in the likeness of Ms. Hall's daughter, Mahji, includes several outfits. Ami, Mahji, Jahmir A Cutout Storybook by Laverne, Velb Associates, 1988, 10½in (26.67cm) dolls. Each doll has several outfits. Keisha the Velvet Touch Fashion Paper Doll with Layered Wardrobe, the Gates Group, 1986, 7½in (19.05cm) paper doll, no tabs, magnets or wax. Clothing sticks by firmly pressing it on doll.
Value: $15, $20, $15, respectively

Li'L Napoleon, *Children's Playmate Magazine*, July 1937, includes 3½in (8.89cm) cutout doll and clothing
Value: $50
Photograph courtesy of Arabella Grayson

Little African Girl (Maya) 1993, *Little Caribbean Girl (Nyla)* 1993, *Little African American Girl (Dana)* 1995, *Naomi the Fashion Model Sticker Paper Doll*, 1997. All are 4½in (11.43cm) by Sylvia Walker, Dover Publications, Inc. Each Dover paper doll contains a short story about each doll to include information regarding her culture. Several outfits are included in each book.
Value: $500

Keisha, Magic Attic Club, 1997, cloth 5½in (13.97cm) paper doll with outfits that stay on like magic. *Christmas Paper Doll Greeting Card,* a Division of Hallmark Cards, Inc., 1999, 5½in (13.97cm) paper doll and several outfits. **Values:** $15, and $3 respectively

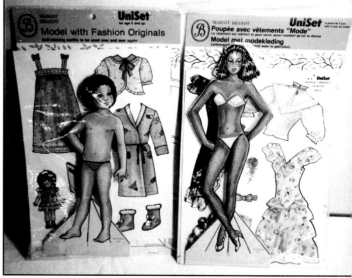

Margit Brandt Model with Fashion Originals #3106, ca. 1990s, a Margit Brandt Design of Denmark; 8in (20.32cm) paper doll on stand, fashions #3009. *Margit Brandt UniSet #3103,* 10in (25.4cm) paper doll with fashion sheet #3003.
Value: $10 each

Kiddoodles Whitney, Peck Aubrey 1996, 6in (15.24cm) doll and outfits sold separately.
Value: $10 (doll) $2 (outfits)

144

Miss America, Golden Book, 1990,
9½in (24.13cm) doll with stand,
precut clothes, fashions to finish,
storage envelope.
Glamour World Paper Dolls,
Checkerboard Press, 1990, 9½in
(24.13cm) young men and 9in
(22.86cm) young women.
Value: $10 each

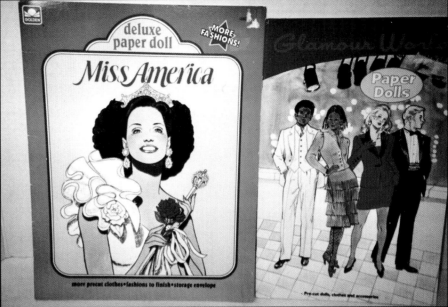

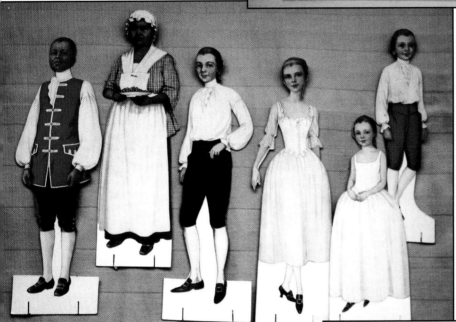

Sukey, the cook and *Moses*, the
butler. Sam'l Gabriel Sons and Co.,
1955, *Sukey*, 10in (25.4cm) die cut
doll with circular stand and one
outfit to cut out. *Moses*, 10¾in
(27.31cm) die cut doll with circular
stand and one outfit with hat to
cutout. Two of a set of six boxed
dolls (included with a Caucasian
family of four, as pictured) titled
Williamsburg Colonial Dolls with
Williamsburg Colonial Dress.
Value: $50
*Photograph courtesy of Arabella
Grayson*

Winking Winny, Whitman/Remco, 1969, 9½in
(24.13cm) doll made in the likeness of Remco's
doll of the same name. Doll, plastic stand, and
press-out outfits included. *Baby Nancy*.
Whitman/Shindana 1971, 9½in (24.13cm) doll
made in the likeness of Shindana's first doll,
Baby Nancy. Doll with plastic stand and 23-piece
press-out wardrobe included. *Magic Mary Jane
Magnetic Paper Doll*, Milton Bradley, 1975,
includes 10in (25.4cm) doll with stand and
several "magnetic" outfits.
Value: $25 each

Doll Families

Brother and Sister Dolls, and Boy Dolls

This chapter is devoted to dolls manufactured within one doll line or series, dolls marketed as brother and sister dolls, and boy dolls. Some of the dolls presented as brothers and sisters may be categorized as such by the author and not necessarily manufactured as such. In all cases, however, the dolls categorized together are from the same series, family, and/or were produced by the same manufacturer/artist.

DOLL FAMILIES

Chatty Cathy® Family

(Left to right, front) *Tiny Chatty Baby®* (1962), reissued *Chatty Cathy®* (2001), *Chatty Cathy®* (1961), and a dyed, formerly white/brunette *Chatty Cathy®*. **Values:** $140, $50, $1000, and $200 respectively

Crissy® Family by Ideal™

All dolls are 18in (45.72cm) with the exception of 15½in (39.37cm) *Tara*® and *Velvet*®, 12in (30.48cm) *Cinnamon*® and 24in (60.96cm) *Baby Crissy*®. All dolls have grow-hair mechanism in center of heads with exception of *Magic Hair Crissy*®.

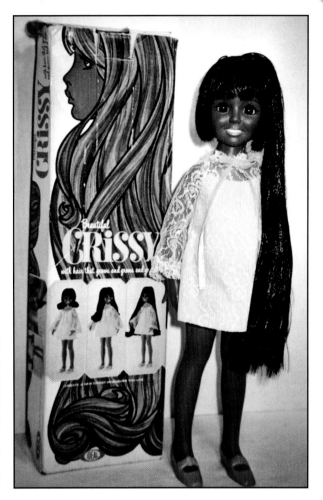

Crissy®, 1970 (box date), wears original green lacy dress, green *Crissy*® shoes with original box and instructions. Doll has black, pupil-less sleep eyes.
Value: $350

Crissy® **Doll Grouping** (Left to right) *Look-Around Crissy*® (1972), *Crissy*® in orange lacy dress (ca. 1970), *Moovin' Groovin' Crissy*® (1971), *Crissy*® dressed as bridesmaid (possibly redressed, ca. 1970). The white *Crissy*® dolls wore the orange lacy dress and orange shoes; Black *Crissy*® originally wore the green lacy dress and green shoes.
Values: $125, $100, $150, and $75 respectively

Tressy® **Dolls** (Left to right) 1971, mint doll in original gold and white dress, yellow shoes; redressed doll wears *Swirlacurla Crissy*® dress. *Tressy*® uses same face and body as *Crissy*® but has closed mouth and brown sleep eyes.
Values: $300 and $150 respectively

Velvet® **Doll Grouping** (Left to right) *Look-Around Velvet*® (1972) dressed in "On the Lamb," *Beauty Braider Velvet*® (1973), and *Velvet*® dressed in "Ruffled Up." *Velvet*® is *Crissy*® *doll's* younger cousin and made her debut into the family in 1970.
Values: $100, $60 and $100 respectively

Reissued *Velvet*® **and** *Magic Hair Crissy*® (Left to right) 1981 and 1977, respectively.
Value: $75 each

Tara®, 1976, Yellow and white two-piece pants suit, yellow T-strap vinyl shoes. *Tara*® is the only *Crissy*® family doll that did not share molds with other dolls.
Value: $200

Cinnamon® (*Velvet*® doll's little sister, left to right) redressed in outfit similar to the "Curly Ribbons" outfit. Doll on right is mint in original orange and white polka dot outfit, orange vinyl T-strap shoes. **Value:** $150 and $300 respectively

Left: **Baby Crissy**®, 1973, has a reddish brown coloring; arm and leg vinyl is softer than the reissued doll's, wears dusty rose baby doll outfit, has black rooted hair with grow-hair mechanism, black stationary eyes (no pupils) smiling open mouth showing teeth.

Right: **Baby Crissy**®, 1981, reissued, came in pink and white box with cellophane; also sold through Sears Roebuck Catalogue and packaged in yellow and white cardboard box. The Sears box showed a picture of the white *Baby Crissy*® with caption "this box contains black version." It is believed that the Sears version wore a white sun suit trimmed in green and white and that all other reissued dolls wore a white sun suit trimmed in yellow and white. Head and body marks are identical to the 1973 doll with the exception of a "2" that appears after the GHB 2M-5611 on the back. This doll's arms and legs are firmer than the original doll's.

My Size Barbie® Family

(Left to right) Front Row: Dancing *My Size Barbie®* (MSB), MSB redressed in 1950s style poodle skirt outfit, redressed in Sweetheart dress and gloves, redressed as a 1920s flapper, redressed in Solo in the Spotlight outfit.
(Left to right) Back Row: MSB Bride, MSB Ballerina, MSB Angel, and MSB Butterfly.
Value: From $150 up
Photograph courtesy of Debra Richardson

Patsy® Family by Effanbee™

The tiniest doll, front and center, is 5in (12.7cm) *Wee Patsy®* ($15). To *Wee Patsy®* doll's left is 9in (22.86cm) *Patsyette®* ($30), and to her right is an original, 11in (27.94cm), composition *Patsy Jr.®* ($300) On the back row from left to right are: 14in (35.56cm) porcelain *Patsy®* on skates ($150); 14in (35.56cm), *Skippy®*, 16in (40.65cm) *Patsy Joan®*, and 14in (35.56cm) *Patsy* ($60, respectively). Unless otherwise stated, all dolls are vinyl, all are reproductions and wear their original outfits with the exception of *Patsy Jr.® Patsy Jr.®* is *the* doll that prompted Debra Richardson's Black-doll collecting fever.
Photograph courtesy of Debra Richardson

150

Precious Moments™ Doll Family

Children of the World® 8½in (21.59cm) *Aisha*® (far right), of Africa, 1996 and *Mazie*® of America, 1989 (far left). Both are all vinyl with jointed arms and legs; rooted, black curly hair; painted eyes and mouths.
Value: $25 each
Precious Moments™ Collectibles Doll (back center) 15in (38.1cm) girl, vinyl head and hands, cloth body and legs, painted eyes.
Value: $50
Friendship Dolls® by Applause™ (front center) 10in (25.4cm) *Heidi*®. Cloth covered Styrofoam head, stuffed-cloth body, arms, and legs; screen-printed facial features.
Value: $15

Saralee® Negro Dolls - Original and Reproduction

(Left to right) *Saralee*®, Ideal Toys™, 1951; *Saralee*® reproduction doll, *Yesterday's Treasures*® by Collectible Concepts™ (sold through Ashton-Drake Galleries™). Original doll: Vinyl, 18in (45.72cm); brown cloth body with crier voice box; (head marks) Ideal Dolls™; molded black hair, brown sleep eyes, brown eyelashes, open/closed mouth with painted lips and tongue. Ideal-tagged dress, original socks, shoes, replaced bonnet. Reproduction doll: Porcelain head, arms, legs; brown, stuffed-cloth body; 17in (43.18cm); (body marks) Produced under license by Collectible Concepts Corp.™, PO Box 581, Great Falls, VA 22066. Doll image is owned by and used under license from Mattel, Inc.™ ©2001 Mattel. All rights reserved. Molded black hair, brown stationary eyes; open/closed mouth; original yellow dress, white bonnet, socks and shoes.
Values: $300 and $150 respectively

Sasha™ Family

(Left to right) **Caleb**®, **Cara**®, and **Cora**®, ca. 1970s by Sasha Morganthaler - *Caleb*® and *Cora*® are 16in (40.64cm); *Cara*® is 12in (30.48cm). Dolls wear original outfits. *Cora*® doll's shoes are replaced. All have Sasha wrist tags that read: Sasha on front; MADE IN ENGLAND Series on back.
Values: $300, $150, and $200 respectively

Zaninni and Zambelli™ Family

(Left to right) **Patrick**®, unidentified larger girl, and **Julia**®, 1986. *Patrick*® and *Julia*® are 21in (53.34cm), larger girl is 25in (63.5cm). Dolls are vinyl with stuffed-cloth brown bodies and wear original outfits.
Values: $60 (smaller dolls) $75 (larger girl)

Apple Valley™ *Hilarious*® and *Pouty*® doll kits, ca. 2001, vinyl heads, arms, legs; brown, stuffed-cloth bodies; 22in (55.88cm) and 19in (48.26cm); *Hilarious*® boy wears brown afro wig; *Pouty*® girl wears brown wig with two pigtails. Both have brown stationary eyes. *Hilarious*® has open, laughing mouth with two lower teeth. *Pouty*® doll's mouth is in a pouting position; dressed in infant's clothing.
Value: $75 each

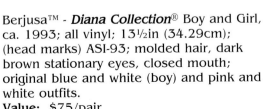

Berjusa™, *Baby Joselle*® (Boy and Girl), 1984; vinyl head, arms, legs; white cloth body; 19in (48.26cm); (Head) Berjusa 53; boy has closely rooted black afro, light brown sleep eyes, open mouth with molded tongue. Girl's hairline on side of face is higher than boy's. Girl also has blue sleep eyes. Boy's outfit is original. Girl's original outfit was identical to boy's except trimmed in pink. Girl is redressed in blue fleece romper made for Lee Middleton™ dolls.
Value: $100/pair

Berjusa™ - *Diana Collection*® Boy and Girl, ca. 1993; all vinyl; 13½in (34.29cm); (head marks) ASI-93; molded hair, dark brown stationary eyes, closed mouth; original blue and white (boy) and pink and white outfits.
Value: $75/pair

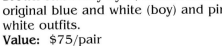

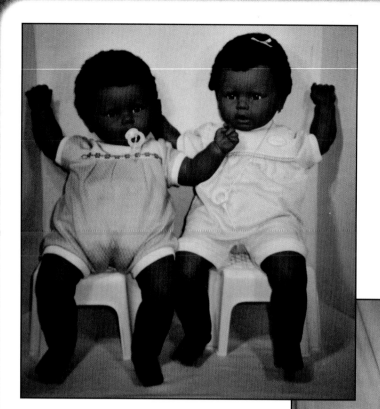

Berjusa™ - *Mi Bebe*® Boy and Girl, ca. 1980s; vinyl, stuffed-cloth body; 27in (68.58cm); (Head) b.b. Spain; closely rooted short afro/brown sleep eyes/open mouths to accommodate pacifier; original clothing with pacifiers that activate their crying mechanism when removed from mouths. **Value:** $100 each

Another pair of *Mi Bebe*® dolls dressed in real infant's clothing.

Faithful Friends™ (Heidi Ott), *Will*® and *Elle*®, 1996; artist type vinyl heads, arms, and legs; stuffed-cloth bodies; 18in (45.72cm). (Head) Heidi Ott's signature incised in back of neck; Kanekalon wigs, brown sleep eyes, smiling mouths with two upper painted-on teeth; original clothing; Dolls were a Target® exclusive, distributed by Dayton Hudson, Corp.™ **Value:** $75 each

Horsman™ - *New Arrival Li'l David*® and *Li'l Ruthie*®, 1975; vinyl head; stuffed vinyl, one-piece body; 13½in (34.29cm); (Boy's head marks) 1/Horsman Dolls Inc/19©75 (Girl's head marks) 8/Horsman Dolls Inc/19©75; molded hair; painted brown eyes; drinker mouth; original outfits. Accessories include yellow pacifier and rattle, white bottles, sponge. These dolls were designed by Irene Szor. They were one of Horsman's first (if not their first) physically/anatomically correct dolls. The outside of boxes contain a message to parents that reads: "This doll has true-to-life features which differentiates little girls from little boys. For those who feel they do not want their children to be aware of these differences, we do not recommend this doll."
Value: $75 each

Horsman™ - *Pete*® and *Polly*®, ca 1950s; stuffed rubber; 13in (33.02cm); 12in (30.48cm); *Pete*® has molded hair. *Polly*® doll's hair is styled in two plaits with bangs. Eyes are molded, painted black. Open/closed mouths with molded teeth and tongues. *Pete*® wears one-piece romper with red and white top. *Polly*® wears light green sunsuit. *Pete*® and *Polly*® were made by Horsman™. The Dee and Cee Company™ also made dolls using this mold. Dolls have authentic-looking, broad facial features.
Value: $150 each

Kingstate™ (Prestige Collection) – *Josh*® and *Josie*®, ca. 2000; baby powder-scented vinyl, jointed head, arms, legs; 17in (43.18cm); (head marks) D'Anton/Jos Spain; molded hair, stationary eyes with upper lashes, open/closed mouths; original hat and diaper. Dolls are anatomically correct, come with birth certificates.
Value: $40 each

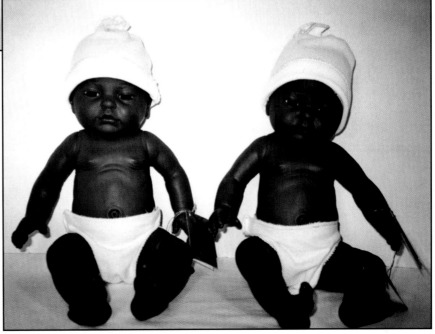

Mattel™ - *My Child*® Boy and Girl, 1985; felt-type cloth; 14in (35.56cm); (body tag) Mattel, Inc.™ 1985/Made in China; boy has short, straight, black rooted hair; girl has long, dark brown, rooted hair, plastic brown eyes, stitched mouths; All original clothing except shoes.
Value: $40 each

Lorna Paris Designs™, Commonwealth - Brother and Sister, 1993; soft-sculptured vinyl; 13in (33.02cm); black yarn hair, screen-printed face; dolls wear tan and black African-print outfits.
Value: $30 each

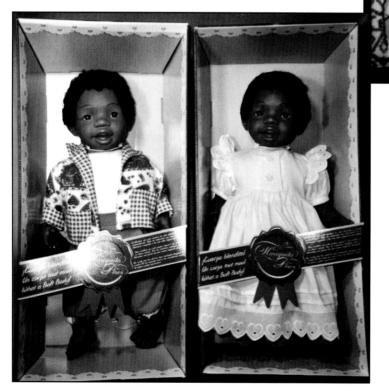

Mariquita Perez/NP Creations SL™ - Made in Spain; Brother and Sister, ca. 1995; artist vinyl head, stuffed-cloth body; 17in (43.18cm); (Head) NP 95; black, rooted, short, curly "afro" style; brown stationary eyes with applied lashes; open smiling mouth with sculpted tongue. All original outfits.
Value: $75 each

Sandy's Dolls™, *Sarah's Gang™ **Willie**®* and ***Tillie**®*, 1995; vinyl; 11in (27.94cm); (Head) 1995 ©Sandy Dolls, Inc. Made in Philippines; rooted black hair, painted brown eyes, closed mouth; original clothes. Each doll comes with storybook that teaches a life value. *Willie*® doll's book is about respect; *Tillie*® doll's is about sharing.
Value: $25 each

FayZah Spanos for Artist Collectibles – ***Vaughn**®* and ***Vanessa**®*, ca. 1993; vinyl with stuffed cloth bodies; 20in (50.8cm). (Head) Baby Ballerina Fayzah Spanos ©1991 Artist Collectibles; black, short curly wig; brown, stationary eyes with applied upper and painted lower eyelashes; open/closed smiling mouth with molded tongue and two upper and two lower teeth; original clothing. These dolls use the same mold as *Buttercup*® (see page 123 top right).
Value: $250/pair

Special Welcome/Cititoy™ - ***Marcus**®* and ***Megan**®*, 2000; vinyl head, hands, feet; stuffed and weighted, brown cloth body, upper arms and legs; 20in (50.8cm); (head marks) ©1997 Cititoy/BS 118 China/GF18; reddish brown rooted hair, brown stationary eyes, applied upper eyelashes, open/closed mouth; original clothing. Doll's have voice box with recording of a real infant cooing. Voice is activated when doll's body is touched.
Value: $50 each

Unmarked Drink and Wet Boy and Girl, ca. 1960s; soft vinyl face, rigid vinyl bodies; 25in (63.5cm); (boy) Molded, black hair/brown sleep eyes/drinker mouth; (girl) black, rooted hair/brown sleep eyes, drinker mouth; redressed in infant's clothing. Boy is made of a darker brown vinyl than the girl, probably made by different manufacturers.
Value: $65 each

Virginia Erhlich Turner – **Tyler**® and **Tasha**®, ca. 1996; vinyl head, arms, lower legs, stuffed cloth, weighted bodies and upper legs; 26in (66.04cm); (head both dolls) Virginia E. Turner (signed and incised in head) #42/500 and #41/500 (written on Tyler, Tasha, respectively); black curly wigs, brown stationary eyes with applied upper eyelashes, painted lower eyelashes; closed, pouty mouths All original outfits, leather baby shoes.
Value: $250 each

The Boys

Special Welcome™ - **Jarred**®, 2001; Val Shelton, Vienna Collection™ **Sleeping Infant**®, 1991; vinyl head, arms, and lower legs; cloth body; 19in (48.26cm) and 20in (50.8cm); Jarred® (Head) 1998 Cititoy BS192 China GF18; Val Shelton Sleeping Infant® "Caleb" (Head) 1991 Val Shelton Vienna Collection; (Jarred) Straight brown rooted hair, brown stationary eyes with applied lashes. (Infant) Auburn wispy wig, closed eyes with applied lashes. Both boys wear yellow outfits. (Jarred) is baby powder-scented and has a voice box. When stomach is squeezed, he babbles in baby talk, laughs, cries, coughs, says mama. "Caleb" was named by the author.
Value: $50 each

Apple Valley™ *Chris*®, 36in (91.44cm); vinyl, cloth body with armature; (head marks) "Chris" ©1995 Pat Secrist; made from an Apple Valley™ doll kit.
Value: $150

(Berjusa) B.B. (Spain) *Coochie Coo*® (mechanical) Boy, ca. 1980s; soft vinyl face, arms and legs; rigid vinyl body that has swivel waist; 28in (71.12cm). (Head marked) B.B. Spain; black rooted afro, light brown sleep eyes, open/closed mouth with pink lip color; blue sweater with yellow, green, and red stripes; blue knit shorts, white socks, black lace-up vinyl shoes. Doll is a battery-operated talker. Speaks in Spanish.
Value: $200

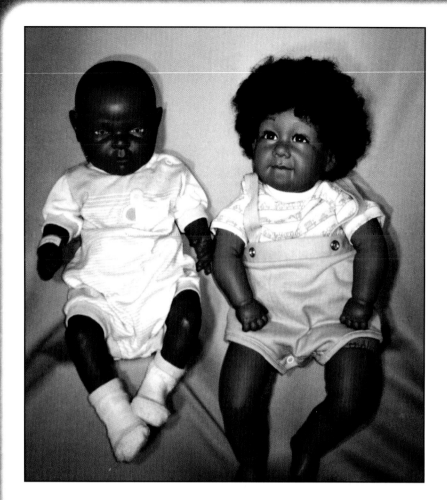

(Left to right) Berjusa™ **Anatomically Correct Infant Boy**, ca. 1980s; Apple Valley® doll kit - **Bubba®**, 2000; (Berjusa) all vinyl with jointed arms and legs; 21in (53.34cm) (Head) Berjusa; molded hair, light brown stationary eyes. (*Bubba®*) vinyl head, arms, legs; brown cloth body; 22in (55.88cm); (Head) Mylo Pat Secrist 1993; brown afro wig, dark brown stationary eyes/applied eyelashes. Both boys dressed in infant's 0-3 months knit romper, disposable diapers.
Value: $50 and $95 respectively

Great American Doll Company™ - *Ricardo®*, Rotraut Schrott, 1990. Breastplate marked: Ricardo/an original/Rotraut Schrott/ Design/The Great American Doll Company ©1990/Anaheim California 92806. 29in (73.66cm), all original clothing.
Value: $350

Lee Middleton Original Dolls™ - *Honey Love Boy®*, 1996; *Little Scottie Girl®* (dressed as a boy) Lee Middleton/Reva Schick, 1997. Artist vinyl head, hands and feet; brown cloth teddy bear-jointed body; 21½in (54.61cm) (*Honey Love® doll's* head) 01596 ©Lee Middleton 1996, hand signed and numbered "Lee Middleton 446/2000"; (*Little Scottie* doll's head) 072197 ©1997 Lee Middleton Original Dolls by Reva (signed by Reva) 1082/1500 (handwritten in ink). (Both) Brown straight wigs, brown stationary eyes, applied lashes. *Honey Love®* — all original. *Little Scottie®* redressed in infant's size 6-9 months outfit with cloth infant's sneakers. *Little Scottie®* doll's original outfit consisted of a red/black tartan plaid skirt, matching scarf and tam, white knit blouse, white tights, and black patent-leather shoes.
Value: $150 each

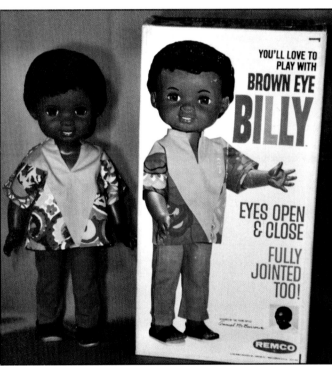

Remco™- *Brown Eye Billy®*, 1969; all vinyl, jointed arms/legs; 16½in (41.91cm); (Head) 3311/U13/REMCO IND. INC.1969; black rooted short curly afro, brown sleep eyes, open mouth with teeth. Features are ethnically correct. Doll designed by African American artist, Annuel McBurrows, whose picture and autograph appear on front of box. All original clothing.
Value: $100

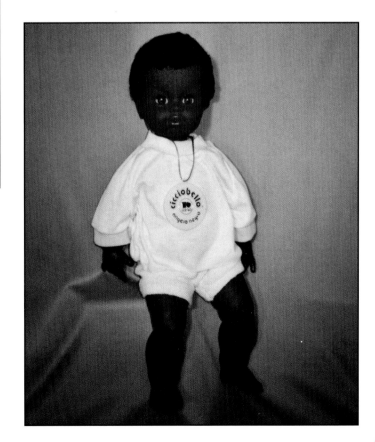

Sebino™ - *Cicciobello Angelo Negro®*, 1979; vinyl head, arms, and legs; tan cloth body; 19in (48.26cm); (Head) Sebino ©Made in Italy. Hangtag reads: Cicciobello Sebino Angelo Negro. Front of cloth body: Cicciobello ilgioco deliaffetto, Prodotto Originale, ©1979 Sebino, made in Italy; closely rooted black curly hair, brown sleep eyes, pacifier mouth; replaced white knit top, possibly original white terry cloth shorts. Doll is mechanical with voice box; sleeps silently when laid to rest; laughs when picked up.
Value: $75

Dolls As Therapy

Have your family and friends wondered about your doll collecting? Do they see it as a juvenile fascination? Accuse you of trying to indulge in childish pastimes?

The most intrinsic value of doll collecting is the soothing therapy that it provides to the soul. We indulge our senses with radiance, wonder and sometimes whimsy when we gather our beauties before us. We are at once kindled with the fire of renewal. Dolls ignite our psyches with the healing warmth of our once childhood play pals, now adulthood treasures.

Dolls allow us to nurture and be nurtured. Remember how often your own little dolly needed your undivided attention as you bathed, dressed, fed and tended him or her by the hour. Now that nurturing is returned to you twice-fold, bringing back the nostalgia of childhood and the wonder of that memory. Were you ever really that young? Were you really that carefree? Yes. Yes, you were. Dolls elicit the same simple-hearted beauty and delicacy again.

Spending precious moments with lovely dolls and all of their tiny accouterments can transcend all the responsibilities and challenges of daily life. Suddenly you find yourself graced by the restorative charisma of the doll, rediscovering inner solace and satisfaction with one of the simple pleasures in life - "playing" with dolls. Only this time, "playing" can mean refurbishing and displaying as well as dressing. What does it matter that the kitchen floor needs a coat of wax or that the boss was in a foul mood again today or that little Tommy wants to have his ear pieced when you can come inside and play? That floor can wait, tomorrow is another day and little Tommy can have his ear pierced - just as soon as he is able to afford his own place! It does not matter when you are playing.

So, when your family and friends accuse you of indulging in childish pastimes, look them straight in the eye and say, "Yes. Yes, I am."

Unknown Author

This poem has been circulated on the Internet. It so vividly describes the feelings experienced by doll collectors that the author felt it appropriate to include it in this section of the book, which is devoted to dolls as therapy.

"Colorizing" (Dyeing) Dolls

How was this done? With Rit® clothing dye (a combination of dark brown, cocoa, and tan) to achieve the desired color of brown for the dolls. For the surfaces that required painting, the area was first primed. Next, acrylic craft paint was used and sealed with a clear varnish. The paint and varnish were applied with makeup sponges. Airbrush painting is also an option.

I have mixed emotions regarding dyeing white dolls Black. If white dolls are purchased for the sole purpose of dyeing brown, manufacturer's may not realize the importance of creating Black versions of dolls. This may also perpetuate their lack of meeting the demands of the Black-doll consumer.

Photograph of the author's dyed specimens, L-R: 1960s *Tammy*, *Baby Thumbelina* with *Penny Brite* seated in front, *Chatty Cathy*, and another *Tammy* dyed a lighter shade of brown.

Kit Dolls

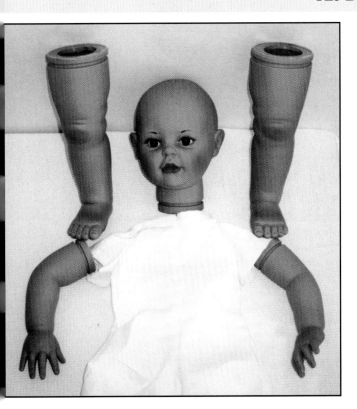

Doll kits are an inexpensive way of creating a doll to your specifications. Whether a novice or a professional, making a doll from a doll kit certainly will provide therapy to the doll maker.

Val Shelton 28in (71.12cm) toddler boy (Sassy mold), 2000, kit includes medium vinyl head, arms, legs; white cloth body. Kit was also available in light and dark vinyl. A choice of brown, green, and blue eye colors were available.
Value: $50

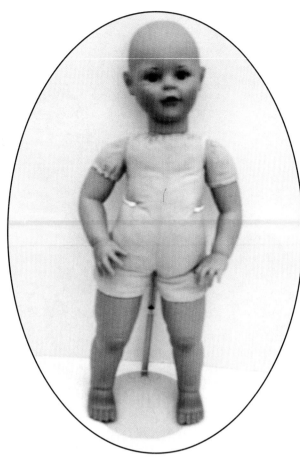

Val Shelton toddler kit (previous illustration) assembled. White cloth body was dyed tan to match the color of the vinyl head and extremities.

Val Shelton toddler kit (previous illustration) completed. Doll wears a size 3-6 months infant outfit.

Completed Val Shelton kits made from the *Sassy* boy and girl toddler and baby molds and the *Pud-N-Cakes* toddler mold, 28in (71.12cm). The baby (girl) has bent legs. The toddlers have straight legs. The dolls were named after author's family members: *Caleb*, *Jewel*, and *Bea*. Dolls wear infant size clothing (3-6 months, 6-9 months, and 12 months respectively). **Value:** $100 each

Other Dolls Made From Kits: See pages 128, 129, 153, 158, 159, 160 and 170.

Reborn Dolls

"Reborn" is a term used for life-size baby dolls that have been customized to look and feel like a real newborn baby. The doll usually starts out as a basic, molded-hair, vinyl, play doll wearing a diaper or basic manufactured romper. Dolls made by Berenguer™ are most frequently used for this process. The "customizer" may choose to add hair (rooted or applied), eyelashes and cheek color. A new infant-style, weighted cloth body is usually added. The doll's nails and/or feet are manicured. The mouth and nasal cavity are opened to give it a breather appearance and to allow for the placement of a pacifier and/or a bottle. The doll is dressed in infant's clothing and renamed. The result is a reborn doll. A birth certificate with the doll's name, date, time, and/or place of birth and weight are also usually created for reborn dolls. An identification bracelet is also often created. Their weights vary in size from 4 to 7 lb. (Sand, water, and other materials have been used to affect the dolls' weight.)

Aaliyah and **Adam** were reborn on August 29, 2001 in Athens, Greece. They have vinyl heads arms, lower legs; cloth bodies stuffed with material used in Greece to fill waterbeds to provide the weighted effect. Both babies weigh 4lb, 7oz. and are 18in (45.72cm) long. They were reborn from play dolls manufactured by Llorens™, sold in Greece. *Aaliyah* has partially rooted and partially applied curly black hair. *Adam* has molded hair. Both have brown stationary eyes with applied upper eyelashes; open mouths with the appearance of a tongue and added facial blushing. Their fingernails have a French manicure. Both dolls wear infant-size clothing, have stuffed teddy bears, and identification bracelets.
Value: $100 each

Buster was reborn from the 17in (43.18cm) Berenguer *Lots to Love™ Chubby* doll in 2001. His arms and legs were shortened to fit an Apple Valley *Num Num™* body, which gives him the chubby infant look and expanded his height to 22in (55.88cm). He is vinyl with a weighted cloth body, has human hair lashes, open nose, and was blushed with paint on arms, legs and face to give him a realistic-looking body color. *Buster* was given two lower teeth and his nails were also painted. He wears infant-size clothing.
Value: $100
Photograph Courtesy of Valerie Ward, NYC

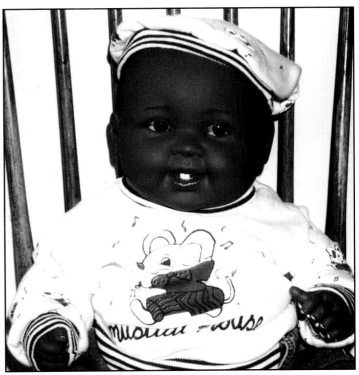

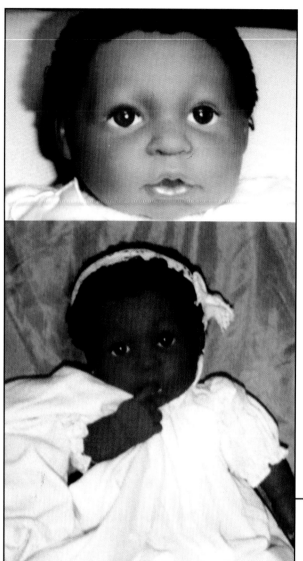

Leif and *Natalie Simone* (top and bottom) were made from the 21in (53.34cm), Berenguer *LaBaby*™ open-eye mold, 2001. *Leif* was born on September 11, 2001. *Natalie* was born on November 2, 2001. Both dolls are weighted with sand to weigh 6lb. Synthetic curly hair was applied, curl by curl. Upper eyelashes were applied; their mouths and nasal cavities were opened, tongues were added, and additional cheek blush was applied. Each doll has French manicured nails. Dressed in infant's clothing, both now reside in Tokyo, Japan via an online auction.
Value: $150 each

I Love Pooh was reborn from a Berenguer *LaBaby*™ sleeping mold, 2001. Doll has applied synthetic curls, Apple Valley™ cloth infant body, vinyl head and limbs. Wears a one-piece, infant's Pooh outfit and has Pooh teddy bear.
Value: $100
Photograph courtesy of Debra Richardson

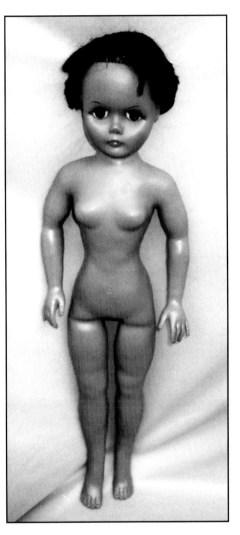

When purchased, this 24in (60.96cm) 1950s, high-heel fashion doll was nude with dry, brittle hair.

Completely made over, the doll in the previous illustration was given a new wig, a new halter-style dress, silver lamé shoes and nylon panties.

The same 1950s fashion doll wears a different wig and outfit. The auburn wig was formerly worn by another doll. The dress is an unaltered majorette cuff found at a thrift store for under $2. The shoes are gold lamé high heels.

Restoring A 1920s Composition Doll

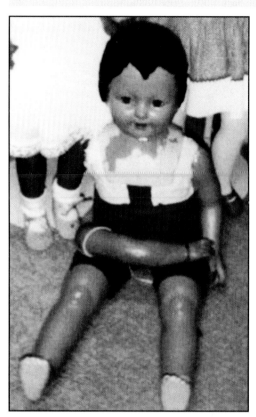

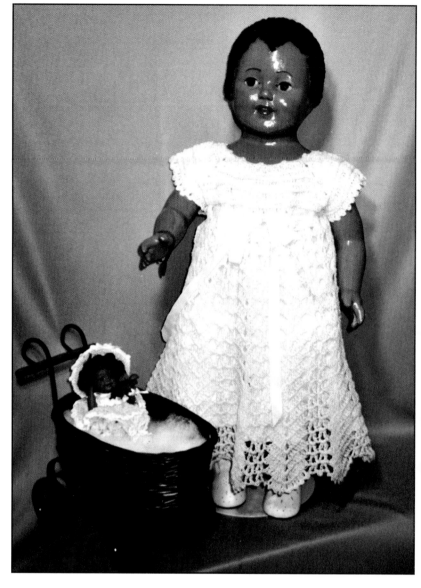

Marilee, ca. 1920s by Effanbee™ is a 23in (58.42cm) composition doll with stuffed cloth body and a ma-ma voice mechanism—an online auction purchase. In the online photographs, similar to this illustration, the doll appeared to be authentically Black. Because it was described as an Effanbee™ and wore its Effanbee™ *Durable Dolls* bracelet, I had to have it and bid accordingly!

Surprise, surprise, surprise! Upon receipt of *Marilee*, it was evident that the doll was originally white and had been half-painted brown, just enough to appear to be authentically Black in the online photographs. The doll's pupils had also been removed, which was not described by the seller and could not be seen in the online photographs. *Marilee* was also nude with one arm detached.

I completed the brown painting, enlarged the lips with red paint to give it a more ethnically-correct appearance, and sealed the paint with acrylic glaze. Brown pupils were added. *Marilee* was then dressed in a yellow crocheted dress, off-white stockings and off-white shoes.

It is not known whether or not Effanbee™ actually made a Black doll using the *Marilee* mold; however, the author now owns a one-of-a-kind version. The smaller doll in the reproduction wicker buggy is a 5in (12.7cm) reproduction *Hilda* doll, *Little Miss Sunshine* by Patricia Loveless. See Chapter 1, Bisque Dolls, page 10 top photo.

The moral of this story: Acquiring dolls via online auctions can be fun; however, bidder beware. Before bidding on online auctions, email the seller and ask questions; retain a record of the seller's answers. If the seller does not answer your questions to your satisfaction or does not answer them at all, <u>DO NOT BID</u>.

Other Important Online Auction Bidding Tips

An important question to ask a seller: Are there any flaws that are not mentioned in the item description or that are not visible in the pictures?

If the shipping and handling fees are not outlined in the auction, ask the seller in advance. Shipping and handling can be exorbitant in some cases.

Remember: If you are not the high bidder of an auction, another like doll will eventually become available for you. Exercise patience.

Whenever possible, be a last-minute bidder. Why raise the final auction amount by bidding early, only to get outbid again and again before the auction ends?

Have fun. If doll buying at auction causes you stress; don't do it.

Doll Play—Redressing Dolls

Redressing dolls is calming to the soul. Just by changing a wig and/or changing an outfit, an old doll can be transformed into a new one.

Jamaica by Peggy Dey. *Jamaica* has been redressed in a navy blue, teddy bear-print, size 2T, corduroy dress. She wears her original white socks and black patent-leather shoes. A red ponytail holder is added to her hair. (Doll wears original outfit on page 105 top right.)

Jamaica has been redressed once again. Now she wears a size 12-month pink and burgundy romper with her original white socks and black shoes. A white ribbon adorns her upswept curly ponytail.

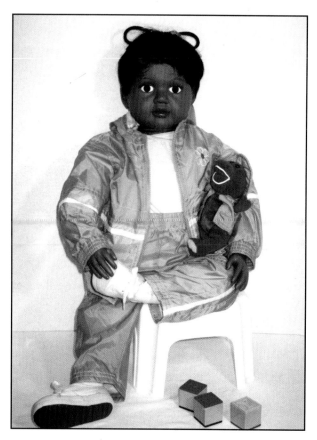

Veronika by Rosemary Rhodes is a fun doll to dress. Here she wears a size 12-month pink jogging suit that matches her pink T-shirt, white socks and white sneakers. She wears her original outfit on page 120 bottom left.

Veronika has swapped outfits with *Jamaica,* see page 169 bottom left. She wears white socks and a child's size 1 leather shoe.

Creating Doll Scenes and Doll Displays

Christine and *Chris* (made from an Apple Valley™ doll kit) eagerly perform their schoolwork.
Photograph courtesy of Debra Richardson

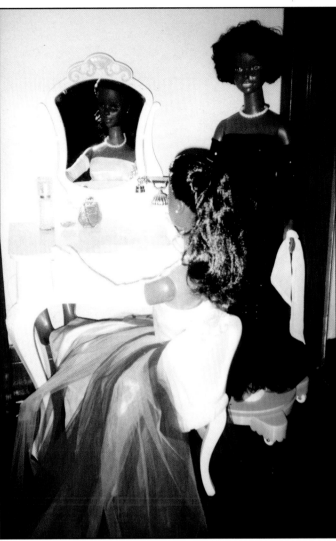

My Size Barbie at her vanity as another MSB waits her turn.
Photograph courtesy of Debra Richardson

Debra Richardson's awesome, well-dressed *Playpal*-type dolls on display.
Photograph courtesy of Debra Richardson

This *Playpal*-type kindergarten class has quietly lined up for recess.

A Christine Orange doll trio patiently awaits mom's arrival after attending Sunday school. *Photograph courtesy of Shirley Scott*

Both girls (**Hannah Rose** and **Hannah Rose** by Kathy McKeon) sit in quiet time after misbehaving. *Photograph courtesy of Shirley Scott and Beatrice Hurt*

Fayzah Spanos dolls sitting pretty: (Left to right) *Me & My Wabbitt, Too!* (2000), *Sugar Plum* (1995), *Sunkissed* (1999) *Ringlets and Rosedrops* (2001), *Tu-Tu Cutie Petutie* (2000). These big, vinyl babies wear their original outfits. All are 26in (66.04cm) tall with the exception of the 30in (76.2cm) *Ringlets and Rosedrops* doll. They make a great portrait! *Photograph courtesy of Manya Elliot*

Doll Accessories

Doll Pins (Left to right) Dolls of Color (DOC) email group pin, WeLoveBlackDolls (WLBD) email group pin, and a Black Doll Collector pin. The DOC and Black Doll Collector pins were designed and created by Zenobia Holiday, moderator of the DOC group. The author designed the WLBD pin, and is the moderator of the WLBD group. See a vintage doll pin, page 13 bottom left.

Other doll accessories available for collectors include doll earrings, necklaces, throws, wall hangings, and wreaths.

Dolls for the Young and the Old

Black dolls are positive images. They reflect Black beauty. Black dolls and playthings allow Black children to see themselves in a positive light. This promotes self-esteem and self-worth. Black dolls as playthings for children of other ethnicities can promote diversification and acceptance.

Dolls have been shown to provide comfort to the elderly, especially for those suffering from Alzheimer's disease. The soothing comfort dolls provide, their ability to promote self-esteem, self-worth, and diversification affirms the fact that you are never too old to play with, admire, or collect dolls.

Black-doll collecting — it's a beautiful thing!

INDEX

"Bea" 164
"Caleb" 164
"Great Lives Observed" 130
"Historic Tradition of Black Women" 130
"Magic Skin" Baby 25
"Petunia" 109
1950's High-Heel Fashion Dolls 67, 167
40th Anniversary Barbie, Ken 42
Abilogu, Roxann D. 28
Adashia 132
Adora Dolls, Name Your Own Baby 71
Adora Rose 120
Aimee 127
Alexander,Madame 22, 65, 69-70, 72
Allied Eastern 71-72
Allied 19
Althea 34
Alysa - Simply Chic, Tropical 55
Amazing Ally 85
Amber 112
American Character 14
American Classic-Lottie 73
American Girl Addy 86
Amity 107
Amosandra 18
Andrews, Ingrid 29
Andy and Mandy Organdy 28
Angel Face 74
Angel Kisses Boy and Girl 117
Angelica 108
Apple Valley 153, 159, 160, 170
Asha, African American Collection 54
Asha 4, 54-55
Ashton Drake 66, 113, 126
Augioletta 116
Australian Boy, Girl (Karda) 81
Avon Representative Barbie 42
Avon Tender Memories Collection-Girl Scout and Batter Up 73
Ayoka 111
Baby Brother Tender Love 83
Baby Catch-A-Ball 96
Baby Crissy 147, 149
Baby Dee Bee 90
Baby Dolly Surprise 86
Baby Georgia 119
Baby Joselle 153
Baby Kimmie 92
Baby Mo 111
Baby Nancy 89
Baby Skates 83
Baby Sunny Boy 112
Baby Zuri 89

Baby-Sitter's Club Jessi 82
Barbie 41-53
Bebe Lollipop Girl 56
Bella 105
Belle, Ashle 74
Beloved Belindy reproduction 35
Benjie 24
Bent Knee Head-Turning Walker 27
Berjusa 74, 153-154, 159-160
Beth 118
Bisque Baby, ca. late 1940s 8
Black Americana Girl 35
Black Barbie 51
Black Licca (Takara) 95
Bonnie-Lu 24
Boudoir souvenir-type 11
Boutique Fashion Doll 57
Brandy 135
Brianne 113
Brown Eye Billy 161
Bubba 160
Buddy Lee 27
Buttercup 123
Cabbage Kid-type 35
Cabbage Patch Kids 33
Cabbage Patch Talking Kids 75
Camisha 116
Candi 55-56
Cara 47, 152
Carol 68
Cassie 34
Celluloid Doll Pin 13
Celluloid Dolls 11-13
Celluloid souvenir-type 13
Ceramic boy and girl, 1930s reproduction 9
Charisse 55-56
Chatty Cathy 146
Chris 159, 170
Christie 51, 53
Christine (Apple Valley) 170
Christine (Beatrice Wright) 97
Cicciobello Angelo Negro 161
Cinnamon 147, 149
Cissette 69
Cissy 69-70
Cloth 28-40
Cobabe, Laura 103
Colette Bride 68
Companion Doll 86
Composition Dolls 14-17
Connie and Danny 74
Coochie Coo 159
Cora 152
Corine(Corina) 123
Cotton Pickers 15
Craft Boy and Girl, Doll Craftin' 18
Crafty Sisters 29
Creedy, Berdine 103
Crissy 147

Cupcake 129
Curtis 47
Cynthia 22
Daddy's Long Legs(Honey/Willie, Slats, Wildwood Will) 103-104
Daisy 61
Dale ,Fab Fashion Fun Denise (Checkerboard) 74
Dale, Van (Topper) 96
Danielle 102
Dasia 57
Davies, Jane 28
Debutante 14
"DebZee" 113
Destiny the Doctor 58
Destiny's Child 134
Dey, Peggy 105
Diana Collection 153
Diana Ross 134
DiMauro, Jeannie 8-9
Dionne ("Clueless") 135
Disco Wanda 90
Doll kit dolls 129, 155, 158, 159-160,163-164, 170
Doll pins 13, 173
Dolls by Jerri 114
Dolls from Kenya 33
Dolls of the World Barbie 47
Dolly Sisters,The 12
Donna 31
Dot 129
Dreamy Walker 90
Duck House 105
Dyed "colorized" dolls 163
E.I.H., Co. (Horsman) 15
Eboli 114
Effanbee 9, 14, 133, 150, 168
Ella 96
Elle (Jakks Pacific) 61
Elle, Wille "Faithful Friends" 154
Elmo 129
Engrid 115
Esme 62-64
Eternal Love Bride 126
Ethiopian Boy 107
Evening Extravaganza Barbie 46
Fashion Dolls 41-70
Fashion Fling Janay, Tariq 58
Fatou 111
Faye Frumpkin 31
Feigenspan, Bettina, 105
Filipo (Dribble Baby) 116
Florence 76
Folk Art Dolls 37
Forek-Schmahl, Marion 106
Francie, Wild Bunch 47
Free Moving Cara, Curtis 47
French Child Doll 25

G5 Vanessa 58
Georgetown Collection 106
Georgette-type 99
Georgiana 33
GI Jane 78
Giggles 80
Gipps, Jan 107
Gone Platinum Barbie 46
Good-Kruger, Julie 107
Googly-eyed 13
Gotz 77, 108, 116
Grace 117
Great American Doll Company (GADCO) 121, 160
Grobben, Joke 108
Hamilton, Helene 55
Hannah Rose 172
Happy Holidays Barbie 48
Hard Plastic Dolls 20-27
Harley-Davidson Barbie 48
Hattie and Her Teddy 101
Heath, Philip 108-110
Henderson, Jean (Expressions of Color) 30
Herman Pecker Dolls 79
Hertel, Schwab & Co. 9
Hilda, reproduction 10
Hilarious 153
Hiliary 118
Himstedt, Annette 111-112
Hitchcock,Kathryn 113
Honey Love Boy 161
Horsman Musical Baby 79
Horsman 34, 155
Ideal 25, 134
Imani Kente Fun 59
International Candi 56
Island Fun Christie, Steven 49
Islander Doll 32
Jackson, Cliff 113
Jacob 113
Jahmelia 119
Jamaica (Kelly RuBert) 105
Jamaica (Peggy Dey) 105, 169
Jamal 42, 54-55
Jarred 158
Jasmine 125
Jessica 4
Jessie Collection 80
Josephine 128-129
Josh 155
Josie 155
Joy Christmas Doll 101
Julia(Diahann Carroll) 136
Julia and Patrick 152
Junior Dallas Cowboys Cheerleaders-Dominique 103
Kacie 30
Kaila 29

Katiba 106
Katrina 132
Keisha Dolls-Keisha, Makeda, Ronnie 82
Kenyata 124
Kerry 112
Kewpie-type 12, 20
Kim Jeans'N Things 91
Kimberly 95
Kwanzaa Dolls (Swansea Dolls) 34
Lars, Byron Runway Series 43-44
Lars, Byron Treasures of Africa 45
Laurie (Unicef Kids) 33
Leanna 103
Lee Middleton Originals 118, 161
Lee, B. K. 115
Levening, Monika 115
Li'l David 155
Li'l Phil 27
Li'l Ruthie 155
Li'l Souls Family-Coochy, Wilky,Sis,JoJo 91
Lifelike Baby Victoria 72
Lingerie Silkstone Barbie 49
Lissi(Batz) 83
Little Friends Collection 92
Little Karee 92
Little Miss Sunshine 10
Little Penny 136
Little Sala 126
Little Scottie Girl 161
Little Soft Janie 89
Live Action Christie 51
Loren 30
Lossnitzer, Carin 116
Loveless, Patricia 10, 116, 168
Lovie, Heubach reproduction 8
Lucinda 129
Madison Mandela 121
Magic Attic Club Keisha 77
Magic Hair Crissy 148
Malaika 93
Malibu Christie 51
Ma-Ma Doll 21, 26
Mammy with buggy 17
Marcus and Megan 157
Margio of Italy 116
Maria 115
Marilee 168
Mary, the Church Lady 127
Maxi Mod 59
Maya 119
Maybelline 129
McKeon, Kathy 172
McLean, Jan 117
Me & My Wabbitt, Too! 173
Mein Baby - My Baby - Mon Bebe 77
Mel B Spice Girls 134
Memories of a Lifetime-Bride, Groom, Cool Cathy 72
Mercedes 128
MiBebe 154
Michael Jackson 137
Michanou 108

Middleton, Lee 84, 117-118, 161
Midnight Tuxedo Barbie 50
Millennium Princess Barbie 48
Molly 128
Morris, Mari 31
Moza (Unicef Kids) 33
Muhammad Ali 133
My Baby 84
My Child 156
My Own Baby 117
My Real Baby 78
My Scene Madison 59
My Size Barbie 150, 171
My Twinn 85
Myrtis 101
Nadia 28
Nafu 28
Naomi Campbell 135
Naomi, Ellisse 60
Ndebele Initiation Doll 118
Nebi 102
Nichelle 42, 54-55
Nubia 84
Nut Head Family 37
Oil Cloth Doll 37
One and Only (Zambardon) 98
Orange, Christine 118-119, 172
Osdell, Mary Van 128
Osman, Ann 119
Ott, Heidi 119
Pamper's Kid 118
Paper dolls 138-145
Paradise Angel #4 102
Paris (Gone Gold, Grand Entrance Paris, Le Concorde) 65
Paris, Lorna 156
Patsy Family 150
Patsy Joan 150
Patsy Jr. 150
Patsyette 150
Patty-Jo 24
Pedigree-type 22
Pemba 111
Penny and Friends 96
Perez, Mariquita 156
Pete 155
Petunia 109, 129
Pineiro, Martha 120
Playpal-type 97, 171
Playtime Wonder 84
Polly 155
Portia 114
Pouty 153
Precious Moments 151
Prim and Proper 124
Princess House 4
Prissy and Missy 39
Puppy Love 107
Reborn dolls 165-166
Remco 87, 161
Retro Bubble Cut Candi 56
Retro Candi 56
Retro Charisse 56
Retro Ponytail Candi 56
Rheinische Gummi und Celluloid Fabrik Co. 11

Rhodes, Rosemary 120 170
Ricardo 160
Ringgold, Faith 34
Ringlets and Rosedrops 173
Rita Walker-type 22
Roberta Walker 23
Rossellini, Bruno 121
Rubber dolls 18-20
RuBert, Kelly 122
Ruby Radiance Barbie 49
Sanga 111
Sarah Jane 10
Saralee 151
Sasha: Cara, Cora, Caleb 152
Saucy Walker-type 23, 27
Schildkrote(turtle mark) 23
Sebino 161
Seraphina 109
Seymour Mann 115
Shaila 122
Shani 54, 55
Shawana 105
She's Like Me Madison 75
Shellie, Our Fairy Doll reproduction 9
Shelton, Val 122, 164
Shindana Toys, Inc. 88-94
Shirley Temple-type Child Dolls 21
Shonda 68
Shopping Chic Barbie 52
Shoshana II 121
Singing Mimi 87
Sissy 129
Sister Dolls Ballerina 29
Skippy 150
Slade Super Agent 93
Small Wonder 84
Snuggle Ebony 107
Societe Francaise de Fabrication de Bebes et Jouets (SFJB) "Unis France" 7
Soul Anthony 133
Soul Sister 76
Soul Train 76
Souvenir Dolls 38
So-Wee 18
Spanos, Fayzah 123-125, 157, 173
Starlight Dance Barbie 46
Starlight Splendor Barbie 50
Steele, Linda 125-126
Stephanie 110
Sue 99
Sugar Plum 173
Sun Dee 19
Sun Rubber Dolls, 18-19
Sun Ruco,Viceroy 19
Sunbabe So-Wee 18
Sunkissed 173
Sunsational Malibu Christie 51
Sunsational Malibu Ken 51
SuperSize Christie 66
Sweet Pea 129
Sweetie Pie 14
Sydney 2000 Olympic Pin Collector Barbie 51
Tabitha 131
Takiyah 30

Talking Brad 51
Talking Julia 136
Talking Master P 137
Talking Tamu 93
Tamara 113, 126
Tammy Candy Striper 87
Tammy 60, 87
Tangerine Twist Barbie 52
Tanza 63
Tara 147-148
Tasha and Tyler 158
Tejada, Reuben M. 126
Terri Lee 24
Thirstee Walker 79
Tiffany Taylor 67
Tillie, Willie (Sandy's Dolls) 157
Tina Thomas 135
Tiny Chatty Baby 146
Toaster Cover Dolls 40
Tod-L-Tot 18
Tomescu, Titus 126
Tomiko 120
Tonner, Robert "American Models" 68
Topsy Turvy 39, 40
Topsy-type 17, 100
Transitional Dolls 25-27
Treasure 125
Treffeisen, Ruth 127
Tressy 147
Trunk Doll 100
Tung, William 31, 127
Turner, Virginia Erhlich 128, 158
Tu-Tu Cutie Petutie 173
Tyler 106, 158
Tyra 131
Uhura 64
Unicef Kids 33
United Colors of Benetton Christie 52
Uptown Chic 53
Vanessa and Vaughan 157
Velvet 147-148
Venus and Serena Williams 137
Veronika 120, 170
Very Velvet Christie 53
Viceroy 19
VICMA 98
Violet Waters 66
Walking Annette 75
Walter 130
Wanda the Career Girl 94
Washington, Mary E. 130-131
Wee Patsy 150
Wellings, Norah 32
Wiggs, Kaye 131
Wild About You 124
Will 110
Willie and Honey(Daddy's Babies) 103
Wilson, Goldie 132
WNBA Christie 53
Wolleydt, Alice 132
Wright, Beatrice 97
Zaninni and Zambelli 152
Zapf 99, 105

BIBLIOGRAPHY

Cross, Carla Marie. *The Crissy Doll Family Encyclopedia.* Grantsville, Maryland: Hobby House Press, 1998.

Gunther, Beth. *Crissy Doll and Her Friends Guide for Collectors.* Norfolk, Virginia: Antique Trader Books, 1998.

Holland, Thomas W. *The Doll & Teddy Bear Department: Sears Catalog's Doll Pages 1950-1969.* Sherman Oaks, California: Windmill Press, 1997.

Judd, Polly and Pam. *Compo Dolls 1928-1955 Identification and Price Guide.* Grantsville, Maryland: Hobby House Press, Inc., 1994 (second printing)

Judd, Polly and Pam. *Compo Dolls Volume II 1909-1928 Identification and Value Guide.* Grantsville, Maryland: Hobby House Press, Inc., 1994.

Judd, Polly and Pam. *Hard Plastic Dolls Identification and Price Guide, 3rd Revised Edition.* Cumberland, Maryland: Hobby House Press, Inc., 1990 (revised edition).

Judd, Polly and Pam. *Hard PlasticDolls, II Identification and Price Guide.* Cumberland, Maryland: Hobby House Press, Inc., 1989.

Perkins, Myla. *Black Dolls an Identification and Value Guide 1820-1991,* Paducah, KY: Collector Books, 1995 (updated).

Perkins, Myla. *Black Dolls an Identification and Value Guide Book II,* Paducah, KY: Collector Books, 1995.

Smith, Patricia. *Doll Values Antique to Modern, Tenth Edition.* Paducah, KY: Collector Books, 1994.

ABOUT THE AUTHOR

Debbie has been an avid Black-doll enthusiast since 1991. Black-doll collecting led to Black-doll research and the desire to network with others who share her passion. Via the Internet, Debbie founded the WeLoveBlackDolls group in January 2001. She is also a member of the Dolls of Color group. Along with that group's moderator, Debbie is coeditor of the first e-zine devoted to Black dolls, *Black Doll-E-Zine.* For over 1½ years, Debbie was also a writer for *Doll E-Gram's* "Spotlight on Doll Collectors" column.

A home-based quality auditor for a major medical transcription company, Debbie was formerly a medical transcriptionist for 27 years, and she is the former owner of Medical Word Specialist, Inc. A Texas resident, Debbie is also a wife, mother, and grandmother.

Collecting, researching, and networking with others who share her passion for vintage and modern Black dolls is Debbie's favorite pastime.